WHERE SPARROWS COUGHED

Contents

First published in 1989 by Sheaf Publishing Ltd,
35 Mooroaks Road, Sheffield S10 1BX

© Frank Hartley, 1989

ISBN: 1 85048 005 2

IT COULD ONLY have been a mind in need of some sort of treatment that dreamed up the name of Salmon Pastures, the district of Sheffield where I was born and spent the first eighteen years of my life. For should that name conjure up for the reader a mental picture of some rural haven where one might relax amidst the peace and contentment of some idyllic corner of this green and pleasant land, then let me quickly assure you that the reality of it was totally removed from that which the words would suggest.

You begin by looking back at the East End of Sheffield forty years ago and imagining a cul-de-sac about fifty yards long by twenty feet wide with a row of eighteen cramped, soot-blackened houses running down one side of it. Then you add a brick wall twelve feet high, going all the way down the other, completely dominating and overshadowing those dirty little houses facing it.

Put in a cobblestone street surface, rows of outside lavatories in the communal yards, cold attics and dark cellars, lace-curtained front windows, and donkey-stoned front door steps for a bit more content.

Throw in two old gas lamps, iron railings at the end where the canal lay, and heavy industrial plant thumping and bumping day and night, making those pathetic little homes tremble and creak in protest at the continual assault upon their very fabric, and then, superficially, the picture gains a little more clarity.

It cannot hope to portray the reality of living in that vast area of innumerable streets, terraces, alleys and odd corners where we and countless thousands lived. Neither can it show the cramped living conditions in which large families lived, forfeiting the niceties of life, such as privacy, dignity and personal hygiene.

Amongst the muck and oily canals, and the rats and mice, and inadequate light fighting a hopeless battle against the high walls and even higher melting shops spew-

Chapter One

SALMON PASTURES

1

ing out yellow and black and grey clouds of filth.

It hardly exists now because those days are over. A committed Socialist city council, the Clean Air Act, new housing estates and savage economic policies have all taken their toll of it.

So that which remains today bears little resemblance to the East End which we knew. And its vibrant pulse has been replaced by the resented presence of itinerant caravan dwellers who come with the night to temporarily populate the areas we grew up in. Picking clean the rib cage of a slaughtered iron beast. Or the mega-rich developers who snap up the derelict land in order to build their futuristic shopping monuments to the Thatcherite dream of endless consumerism. Neither of them having, or wanting, the slightest concern at what nostalgic sadness their particular cannibalism inflicts upon those old enough to have shared its yester-years. And can hark back, rightly or wrongly, to what once was.

For Sheffield's East End represented a way of life sustained by full employment and a worldwide reputation for its product. A finished material so good that the world queued up to buy it, and you felt proud to be involved. So proud, in fact, that you ignored, or turned a blind eye to, the fact that those who built and owned those steelworks considered you common, with common ways and common tastes. And so they gave us common little houses to live in, love in, fight in and eventually die in.

Well, now it's gone, but the memories remain. Especially if you had a sense of humour, the whole host of characters were a joy to behold. They made us laugh, and laughing was the answer to the anger, despair and bitterness that the housing and dirt and noise germinated.

To share these memories is to share those laughs.

In this 1930s view, the Sheffield-Worksop Railway and Lumley Street are at the bottom of the picture, with the Sheffield Canal immediately adjacent. Looking north, we cross Effingham Road, the River Don and Attercliffe Road before reaching the long viaduct of the Midland Railway.

'PEGGY' COCKCROFT lived four doors below us in Salmon Pastures, and got that name because of his wooden leg. As a small boy my little stomach used to tighten up in fear as I lay in that pitch black front bedroom sharing a bed with my elder brother, Tom, listening to the clumping noise that Peggy's substitute limb made on the flagstones beneath our window as he made his way home each night from the *Dog and Duck* two streets away.

I would burrow my head deep down below the covers and screw my eyes tight shut whilst doing my utmost to get as close as possible to our Tommy. He, of course, took full advantage of my terror by sticking his head down and saying in a mock terrified way that Peggy was on his way up our stairs and was coming to get me.

He later came to regret gaining any cruel satisfaction derived from exacerbating my fear when it began inducing me to have rather violent nightmares. For not only did these nocturnal visitations cause me to scream and hit and kick out wildly upon his sleeping body but also, with deadly accuracy, to relieve myself all up his unprotected back.

Looking back on it I can laugh in justifiable glee at his efforts to remove his soaking wet singlet whilst roaring out his protests to our parents in the back bedroom of how I had 'done it again, mam'.

I venture to suggest that being wakened half-way through the night by someone beside you screaming and lashing out in fear is not an experience that many people would care for.

To have that and your singlet soaking wet and somehow stuck tight between your shoulder blades, with the added indignity of getting the thing off over your head, makes it infinitely worse.

I must point out here that this fear of Peggy was entirely unfounded on my part. In fact, for many years he was afforded great respect and admiration for the manner in which he had sacrificed his leg. It had happened in the Great War on the Somme, when young Albert, his real name, was a mere nineteen years old. He had, with total disregard for himself, crawled thirty yards risking withering enemy machine gun fire to reach and drag back a wounded officer.

Consequently Peggy, because of his heroism, was looked upon with great favour by the whole neighbourhood. There were some who did ponder occasionally as to why he never received any sort of a medal for it, but no one ever stooped to challenge him about it.

He would relate the incident in a regular, if monotonous, way in the *Dog and Duck* dram shop, knowing that by the end of it he would have gained himself at least two free pints.

There would be flickers of doubt sometimes amongst the mainly bored listeners, especially as the story seemed to differ slightly each time he told it, but in the main they would shrug it off and blame it on the shock of being crippled so young in life.

'Theer ah were,' Peggy would shout emotionally as he swayed upon his one good leg. One hand would be clutching the bar rail whilst the other one swooped and swirled the pint he clutched dangerously close to the heads of those sat nearest to him.

His face would be set deadly serious, wild unblinking eyes, and a firmly set mouth. Well, as firm as a mouth can set when all its top teeth are missing, that is.

'The result of a German rifle butt being smashed in me face when I made me escape,' was the answer you would get should you enquire about the missing molars. Anyway: 'Theer ah were,' he'd say, 'alone . . . on me own. All ah cud see was him . . . laid out theer . . . hurt. Reight under their noses he were . . . laid theer . . . like that.'

And then he would bang down his glass

Chapter Two

THE OLD WOMAN FROM STOCKPORT

and stretch both arms before him, letting his head droop forward onto them in demonstration.

'Hey up, Peggy,' a voice would come from somewhere with just a hint of suspicion in it, 'are tha sure it's t'same bloke as last week?'

'Course ah'm bloody sure,' Peggy would snap, lifting his head to peer blearily around for the doubter.

'Well . . . ah wondered like,' came the voice again, 'only . . . for a bloke what's been shot to pieces . . . well . . . he's bloody lively enough . . . in't he? . . . he keeps on changing positions.'

And so it would go on and on. Each grisly detail of his mud-clinging crawl and the badly wounded comrade swearing eternal gratitude and a substantial monetary reward should Peggy get him back alive. The searing hot bullets raking him from hip to toe. (So what if they did go the other way last week? They still hurt, don't they?).

The innumerable times that he fainted from shock, effort and blood loss as he inched his way back to their own lines, somehow dragging the officer with him.

The fury he felt, the shock and revulsion as he looked closely for the first time into the face of the man he had just given his best leg for.

'The same bastard that had charged me the week before for not 'aving enough studs in me boots. Three days' pay ah lost . . . it were 'im . . . t'same bloke.

'Look at this,' he would shout in a final dramatic flourish as he hammered his pint glass against his wooden leg. How many bleeding studs can yer get in one o' these then?'

Now this dram shop ritual would have gone on for ever and a day had it not been for the arrival one day of an elderly lady who came to visit him from Stockport.

She turned out to be his sister, and Mrs Flynn, who lived five doors down from us, took her in for a cup of tea seeing as Peggy was out.

The result of their brief tête-a-tête not only put the mokkers on any possible credence that Peggy might have claimed for his gallant act, it also killed stone dead the Freeman's ale he had been supping for donkeys years.

According to his sister, the nearest our young Albert ever got to France was when he was ten years old and on a day's outing to Scarborough. He had apparently taken it upon himself to insult the crew of a French trawler by showing them his rather unimpressive John Thomas whilst jumping up and down on the quayside shouting 'Wee-Wee'.

His resultant capture by them not only earned him a few hefty kicks up the channel, but also a grade one pasting from his father when he heard about it later.

What about his wooden leg?' we asked Mrs Flynn in astonishment. 'He can't be lying about that . . . that's real enough isn't it?'

'Aye,' she replied grimly, 'and so's that bleeding Blackpool tram wot he fell under when he got pissed up on cider.'

As his sister had pointedly observed whilst putting the facts straight about their young Albert: 'Christ knows how they got a German machine gun nest under there an' all.'

And his teeth? The ones that some vicious Hun had smashed in to foil his patriotic dash to freedom to carry on the just fight?

'Lost 'em at playing rugby,' croaked Mrs Flynn in disgust. 'He were laid down holding t'ball for one o' other lads to score, an' as he run up to kick it a wasp stung 'im an' he kicked Peggy straight in t'gob instead.'

That isolated visit by an old woman that none of us had ever seen before ruined him completely.

Looking back on it at a much later age it seems inconceivable that I could ever have been so frightened of him as a child.

Leading off Attercliffe Road, Clay Street was typical of the East End, terraced houses rubbing shoulders with large and often noisy works buildings. On the other side of the wall at the end of Clay Street is the River Don.

THEN THERE WAS F...F...F...Freddie Thorpe and his wife, Ria, who lived in the first house.

The terrible impediment in his speech was enough to drive any listener to distraction, but to make matters even worse, his wife was affected with a condition which created roughly ten times the normal amount of saliva that an average mouth should hold.

The effect of this was that when she addressed you in conversation it was tantamount to standing in the rain.

Now they always occupied the double seat immediately alongside the coal fire in the best room in the *Dog and Duck*, and woe betide anyone daft enough to sit near them.

Freddie's interminable struggle to get his words out created more nervous tension in there than Hitler ever did.

I've seen pints of beer raised and brought to within an inch of the drinker's mouth, only for the movement to freeze at that point as the drinker desperately willed Freddie to complete what he was trying to say so that he could relax and take a drink.

If you can imagine Freddie, with his face screwed up and his finger pointing at you to emphasise the point he was determined to make, even if it took you all night to understand him, being continually urged on by Ria who couldn't quite understand why you kept ducking, then your sympathies must surely lie with the poor sod caught up in it.

It was bad enough going without a drink until Freddie had accomplished his task, but to have to sit with one hand covering your beer and the other holding your hanky tended to spoil the whole purpose of you being there at all.

Billy Whittaker, who ran the place, was at his wits end at the complaints that came flying over the bar about these two.

'What can I do?' he protested. 'I can't bar 'em just because he stutters an' she spits all o'er every time she opens her mouth . . . can I?'

'Tell 'em to tek their beer an' go an' sit on t'canal bank,' said one irate customer.

'Aye,' said another, 'she can gob all she likes down theer . . . mind, tha'd better tell them down at Tinsley lock to keep an eye on t'watter level.'

'She's been barred from our doctors,' chimed in old Mrs Palmer, who had given up sitting in there after getting so wet one night that she caught a cold on the way home and swore blind she would never risk it again.

'An' she's been barred from Bostocks pork butchers . . . an' she can't go in Owens pawnshop any more either,' she insisted.

Billy was adamant, though, and refused to leave himself wide open to wide-scale criticism throughout the area. He simply refused to bar them or give in to their demands, and so Freddie and Ria remained.

'Has tha' . . . has tha' . . . has tha'...' Freddie began one night to his wife as they sat there. Alone.

'Spit it out, can't yer,' scowled Ria impatiently at him as he screwed up his face in concentrated effort, whilst at the same time drawing the back of his hand across his wet cheek.

'They don't . . . they don't . . . they don't...' began Freddie again in a further attempt.

'What are yer trying to say?' snapped Ria, making Freddie wince and turn his head away at the cascade that hit him.

'We sit . . . we sit . . . we sit . . . we sit...' he tried once more. By this time everyone else in the place had given up any hope of relaxing as Freddie fought his battle with himself.

'For Christ's sake, send her a letter,' grumbled somebody. 'It'll be a lot quicker.'

Eventually, as he always did, Freddie got his statement coherent enough for everyone to understand that what he was trying to say was that he felt hurt that he

Chapter Three

STANDING IN THE RAIN

and her seemed to be shunned by everyone else every time they went in the place.

'Sod 'em,' snapped Ria. 'Sod 'em all.'

And the guilty feelings that most of them had momentarily felt disappeared as they quickly covered their glasses.

I don't know where they are now. When they pulled our houses down and moved us to greener pastures I lost all touch with Freddie and Ria.

But you can bet your life that there's a pub somewhere in Sheffield right now where all the regulars sit with one hand covering their glass.

Two typical Attercliffe pubs. The *Tramcar* (right) stood on the Common at the corner of Clay Street and contrasted with the *Omnibus Inn* (below), on Attercliffe Road, behind which was typical East End housing on Worksop Road.

IF ANYONE COULD HAVE matched or even surpassed that pair for getting other people uptight, then it had to be Sam Duffy. God, in his infinite wisdom, must have taken one look at him and then smashed the mould.

For sheer selfishness, inadequacy and unbelievable skill at getting his neck in a knot, Sam was unassailable. He was the epitome of everything that I didn't want to be, and yet he filled me with admiration at his ability to pick himself up and carry on when lesser mortals would have run away in shame.

Nothing, but nothing, could tear him away from believing that he was the victim of unseen forces, evil in their intent at making his life a misery by heaping one catastrophe after another upon his righteous being. The fact that he unequivocally brought these things upon himself was totally rejected by a mind unable to even comprehend that HE could be in the wrong.

He was completely self-centred, and his total indifference to his wife's feelings or needs was matched only by his overwhelming protection of his own.

His wife, Edna, came from well outside our area and never really settled down amongst our conditions. Although for his sake and that of a daughter they had, she did try.

Actually, she wasn't a bad looking woman, well built with auburn hair and a pair of legs that drew many an admiring glance. Most of us marvelled at Sam's success at landing her, seeing as how his outward appearance could quite honestly have been described as akin to looking into a bucket of lard.

Her upbringing had not been on a level that was any higher than ours, except that her home at Stannington gave her the advantage of actually living in the countryside.

There were times when she would stand on her front doorstep talking to us when we were kids, usually when she was fed up at being left on her own so much.

There would be me, Harry Owen, Herbert Lee, Pete Fairfax and Sammy Gregory all in a bunch around her front door. We'd be about nine or ten years old then, and her descriptions of the Rivelin Valley, the Derbyshire Moors and the views that she missed over Loxley stirred all of us with an urge to see them for ourselves.

She made us realise at a very early age that only a decent tram ride away lay a world where rivers and streams were actually clean, with even live fish in them. There were hundreds of trees and grass for miles, and even wild animals like foxes and rabbits and squirrels and all sorts of things really lived.

We would discuss the possibilities of going to see these things amongst ourselves later whilst throwing stones at an old oil drum stuck fast in the filth of the canal, or perhaps kicking an old tennis ball against that high wall that dominated us.

'Will thi mam let thi go?' Herbert would enquire of all of us, seeing as he realised that his chances were virtually nil.

'Mine will,' Harry would say firmly. 'She lets me go any wheer.'

'Any wheer tha wants?' Herbert would incredulously ask.

'Aaah . . .' Harry would confirm fiercely. 'Ah've been to Cleethorpes, tha knows.'

'On thi own?' we would all gape at him.

'Naow . . . in me Uncle Harry's sidecar wi' me Aunty Mabel,' he would say in disgust at our stupidity.

'I'll tell her that we're just going a walk to Spital Hill an' back,' Pete Fairfax would chime in, drawing his tatty jumper sleeve across his nose for the umpteenth time that day.

I suppose everybody knew someone at some time who had trouble as a kid with a nose that insisted on sending out elongated messages that made everyone else feel sick.

Well, Pete Fairfax was ours, and if I

Chapter Four

SAMUEL DUFFY

should ever forget his name, it's a certainty that I'll never forget that jumper he always wore. It always had one sleeve the bottom of which was hard enough to hammer nails in with.

It was to be a year of two after this before we actually did get to see the things that Edna Duffy fired our imagination with, but I do know that her easy, quiet nature towards us and everyone else gained her much sympathy and admiration at being able to keep her marriage vows intact.

My first memories of them stem from when I was about five or six years old. Sam would have been about twenty then, and I can still see him swaggering down Salmon Pastures.

He had this rolling gait with exaggerated movements of his shoulders which would have drawn admiring glances had he been a sailor, but, seeing as how he was barely five feet two high, and fat with it, his motions were quickly labelled by one wit as 'like watching a monkey with bad feet making love'.

He had married Edna a few weeks previously, and I well remember watching them move into the house two doors up from us. They brought what few possessions they had on Tommy Nesbit's rag and bone cart one morning, with Edna sharing the high seat with Tommy, whilst Sam waddled alongside holding onto the side of the cart.

There was nothing unusual in this method of moving into a house in those days down our way, and Tommy, along with many others of his calling, found their services frequently called upon.

Those of us already living there watched the newcomers' arrival with suspicious curiosity from open front doors, or by furtively peeking from behind carefully held curtains.

Sam and Edna, of course, were fully aware that everything they had, as well as themselves, was being subjected to close scrutiny, and responded in the traditional way by holding their heads high and giving cold stares to anyone they saw.

Tommy Nesbit had decided that he would back the cart down our street seeing as it was a dead-end, and proceeded to demonstrate his skill to us by getting the rather ragged looking black and white pony to go in reverse. This impressive performance was watched by us all for the thirty yards or so it took to reach the house, and Sam made much capital from it by walking ahead uttering loud cries of 'Come on . . . come on,' accompanied by dramatic wavings of his left arm, until finally the brightly coloured cart reached its destination.

Tommy, with loud cries of 'Whoa' and growled threats concerning the beast's immediate future came to a halt.

He looked down disinterestedly as Sam raised his arms to support his new bride as she nervously began her descent from the high perch. Her right foot anxiously sought the small metal step close to the pony's hind-quarters, whilst her hands reached down to grip and dig into Sam's fleshy neck. This made him wince and pull a face beneath his ever-present cap.

The sudden weight of her falling forward onto him as she totally missed the step caused Sam's legs to buckle, and a desperate battle then ensued as Edna, with one leg pumping up and down in mid-air searching for the step, and the other one still frantically clinging to the car, transferred her grip from Sam's complaining neck to envelope his entire head, cap and all, with a vice-like double-arm grip that would have graced any street fight.

Now Sam, who, as I said earlier, was rather small in stature but lacked nothing in fat, found this situation hard to cope with. The fact that his wife was almost horizontal to the cart and that her grip on his head was causing the neb of his cap to bore itself into the bridge of his nose as his feet did a tap dance on the cobbles in his efforts to take her weight, brought the previously bored onlookers alive with interest. Smiles began to appear as Sam's muffled groans and curses were obliterated by Edna's shrieks of alarm. Tommy the ragman just sat there unmoving in his close observation of what was happening below him.

The smiles turned to giggles as Sam's struggling body did its best to support his wife's undignified departure from the cart, and finally to loud laughs as Edna launched herself fully upon him, causing them both to fall in a heap on the new doorstep.

Half the women in our street were out by this time, plus the odd husband here and there, and they abandoned all restrictions like door steps and curtains to crowd out onto the narrow pavement, determined not to miss any of the arrival of the Duffys.

Poor Edna's face was crimson as she frantically extricated her arms, which were trapped under Sam's head, and struggled to her feet, glaring in her fury at the laughing onlookers who were showing not the slightest sympathy.

Angrily, she turned back to look down at the still prostrate body of her husband lying there, and her heart sank even further at the sight of him. He laid there, chest heaving as he gasped for breath, with the neb of his dirty flat cap jammed firmly beneath his nose, so that half of his face was hidden from us.

Edna stooped over him, and with one sweeping movement of her hand simply flipped the cap clear, bringing forth from Samuel a scream of pain so startling that the pony panicked. It set off with such a surge that Tommy was catapulted backwards out of his seat, causing him to become entangled between a bed, a tin bucket, a mangle, a roll of faded carpet and various bags, boxes and other oddments.

Tommy's petrified shouts and commands to the headstrong beast were totally ignored by it as it dragged the bouncing, swaying cart behind it in a charge that would have done justice to any Errol Flynn movie.

Sam and Edna could only stand and stare in disbelief as their pitiful possessions disappeared back whence they came, running over Ria Thorpe's ginger cat in the process.

'Christ,' cackled Mrs Flynn, who was watching all of this with the rest of us. 'I've never known anybody move in and back out of this street so fast.'

Ria Thorpe's cat was writhing about in the gutter with obvious injuries, but no-one would volunteer to go and tell her as they were too engrossed in what was happening.

And then Edna wept.

The sight of her standing there, hands covering her tearful face, as she cried in her embarrassment, and her awareness that what few things they possessed had not only been exposed to the disdainful looks of all those watching, but also had been party to a pantomime for them to laugh at.

Her sobs brought an end to all our enjoyment of the situation, and several women tentatively approached her and began to offer words of sympathy and encouragement, whilst Sam, who had by this time regained his feet and some composure, put a short podgy arm around her shoulders and gave her a comforting hug.

That was a typical reaction from the people that I grew up amongst, tough, quick to be suspicious, quick to laugh at another's misfortune, quick to be scornful, but equally quick to realise that help was needed and therefore offered.

Sam and two other men set off to track down the runaway cart, whilst Edna was ushered into Mrs Flynn's for a sit-down and a cup of tea. She sat Edna at the table in the front room, because she was very proud of her beautiful green velvet tablecloth and wanted to swank. She left the front door wide open, and several of the other women looked in to encourage her as she sipped her tea and felt grateful to them all.

The rag cart duly returned, but there was no sign of Sam or his helpers with it, and so Mrs Flynn and Rosie Crapper, who occupied the next house to the one that Edna had taken and was known the length of our street, and several others for that matter, as 'that bleeding pest in a turban', set to in helping Edna and Tommy Nesbit unload the cart. Not that it wanted much doing, mind you, seeing as what few things there were wouldn't have filled a room, never mind a house.

Nevertheless, Edna and Mrs Flynn set about washing the oil-clothed floors, cleaning the windows and hanging the curtains, while Rosie Crapper chain-smoked and rattled on about everyone's business in the street, until Mrs Flynn, sick to death of hearing her voice and of waiting for Rosie to actually help with the work, deliberately knocked over the heavy metal bucket she was using, causing not only a flood of dirty, soapy water to cascade all over Rosie's feet, but also to cause the rim of the aforesaid receptacle to come down quite heavily across her corn-plagued toes.

As Edna remarked to Sam later (much later, as a matter of fact, due to how he and his helpers had soon tired of looking for the missing cart and had unanimously agreed to have 'just a quick one' in the *Dog and Duck*), when she related this incident to him:

'I've not heard language like that from any woman before in my life, Sam.'

'Yer mean she were swearing bad?' Sam enquired, blearily sprawling back in the one soft covered chair they possessed.

'Aye,' said Edna, eyes wide in shock, 'real swear words . . . yer know . . . like you do at work.'

'In 'ere?' Sam sat bolt upright. 'In our new house? The dirty mouthed old sod . . . don't let her in 'ere again . . . do yer hear . . . we don't need her.'

That dislike for Rosie by Sam was to carry on through many years of living alongside each other, and led to many nasty moments in the Duffy household. Mainly because of Rosie's insistent prying and cadging and Edna's inability to be strong with her.

I suppose, once again, that every street must have had their own Rosie Crapper in one form or another, but I certainly remember ours alright. She never seemed to wear anything different from that perpetual coloured turban, a wrap-over pinafore (usually dirty), house slippers with the toes out, and a Woodbine in the deep-brown stained fingers of her right hand.

Me and the other kids I've already mentioned used to play all sorts of tricks on her as we grew through our early years into young men. I must admit that the memory of Rosie standing framed in her open doorway on a dark night with the light from the solitary bare bulb hanging behind her in their front room emphasising all the mistakes in her bodily construction — which her long-suffering husband Gus often drew attention to whilst drinking — as she bellowed out a string of obscene threats of what she would do upon our personages should she catch us, is one that is indelibly imprinted upon my mind.

To hear a woman use 'them words', especially aloud in the street, was well worth the risks we took in tormenting her, even if we did tremble with fright sometimes as we hid in the dark entries away from her searching gaze.

Happy days. Well in our own limited way they were. To be young, small enough to hide, and fast enough to escape when a prank went wrong. Tying a length of rope to a back door and the other end to the handle of an outside lav in the inky black backyard and then inwardly screaming in mirth as the victim cursed and blasphemed trying to answer the loud knock one of us had performed to rouse them.

Fastening tin cans to cats' tails then following its frantic dash through dozens of entries and yards as it made a hell of a din.

Getting your mother to knit a pair of

swimming trunks to go to Attercliffe baths in. Then discovering that water not only makes them weigh a ton, it also invariably ripped them off each time you dived in. God, the number of times the attendant ordered us out for having bare bums in mixed bathing. They stopped us going in at the finish unless we had 'proper' costumes because our home-made ones were blocking all their filters up.

Great times, and good laughs from these and other things, and from the people that we lived amongst. 'Peggy' and the Thorpes and nosey Rosie and old Mrs Flynn and many, many more. Each and every one of them impressing themselves upon a young mind which, in later years, feels a great nostalgia in remembering them.

I wasn't there on the day that they all locked their doors for the last time to move out into 'posh' council estates. I was abroad . . . as a soldier.

But when they left they took much more than just their furniture and effects with them, they took that unique camaraderie with them as well. It would never re-create itself again in their new environment. It would die as they enjoyed the new luxuries of indoor lavs, your own bath, enough bedrooms and a garden to grow vegetables in.

Goodbye Salmon Pastures . . . hello privet hedges.

I was sixteen when King George VI died, on 6th February 1952. Much to our irritation, the wireless promptly gave itself over to miserable chamber music for the rest of the day, and I was completely baffled by our Works Manager, who announced to us all that, 'The King is dead, long live the King'.

The days following were gloom-laden, with papers and newsreels filled with pictures of the lying-in-state and the funeral (to which came no fewer than six kings), and the country learned a new word: *catafalque*.

The Coronation was eighteen months later, in June 1953, and there were street parties and municipal bonfires and some working men's clubs even gave away free beer. But for many people, the most exciting news that day was that Sir Edmund Hilary and Sherpa Tensing had climbed all 29,002 feet of Mount Everest. Now that *was* something.

In Works And Streets A Silence Fell

THE moment arrives, and the heavy hammer in a Sheffield steelworks is stilled. With heads bare and bowed, the crew stand stockstill, and remember in a silence broken only by the hissing of steam and the roar of the furnace. At 2.02 p.m. the great hammer begins to pound again. Below is the scene in Fargate, Sheffield, during the silence.

Stillness Came To The Forges

TEN minutes to two. Sixty-eight-year-old Frank Trumper, senior foreman of the East Gun Forge of Thos. Firth and John Brown Ltd. and 50 years a steelworker, looks at his watch.

"I've just checked it," he shouts though he stands beside me. There is a fierce hiss of steam escaping at high pressure. A crane rumbles overhead carrying a red-hot bar of steel in its sling. A sudden wave of warmth sweeps over us as it passes.

GROUND QUIVERS

The dirty building seems to be filled out with all but with deep, shuddering sound. The ground is quivering. From the furnace comes a terrific heat.

To the right a fiery body moves. One holds a long-bar comes down. The bar of steel is in the cutting busy shoots.

He looks at... minutes to the signal silence is here.

From the... men that... comes a... ing of an... sorbered...

WAVE

Foreman goes... bar of steel... their five-foot... Too whose... waves his... the forge... machine... stand...

Prince Hur...

RETURN...

THE Marchioness... her 20-year-old... Blackwood, who... Margaret, were bot... crashed as they wer... funeral at Windsor...

Their car struck a la... the Great West Road, a...

Train Is Wrecked, So Zone Ban On

CANAL ZONE, Frida... BRITISH forces reimpos... their security block... on the Suez Canal... tonight after Egyp... terrorists using mines... wrecked a British Army... train.

Gen. Erskine said that... cord blocks and check poin... be set up again on the mai... Said-Ismailia highway.

Further releases of... auxiliary policemen, he... British troops storm... Ismailia barracks on... 25, will be postponed.

"Consideration will... tomorrow," said Gen. E... stopping all Egyptian... throughout the Canal... the Egyptians clear... wreckage.

The mines, electri... ated, wrecked the... caused two craters... and 10 feet in dian... soldiers with the... with minor injuries.

RIOTS D...

The Egyptian... plying to the... tion denied t... official commu... tion of Janu...

The Ge... which Stan... sened, has... source f...

The... Minis... Linds... Shef...

PUBLIC NOTICES

CORONATION DAY BAND PERFORMANCES at 3 p.m. and 7 p.m. in:—
Endcliffe Park
Hillsborough Park
Concord Park
Graves Park
Millhouses Park
Beaver Hill Recreation Ground (Woodhouse)
Bole Hills Recreation Ground.

FIREWORKS DISPLAYS (Weather permitting) at 10 p.m. in:—
Norfolk Park
Meersbrook Park
Longley Park
High Hazels Park.

City of Sheffield Parks Department.

OF THE MEMORIES that I can recall of those short days between me leaving school and getting called up into the army, none bring back a more pleasurable warmth than the visits to the old *Empire Theatre* on Charles Street.

The war was over, street lights were back on again and flashing neon signs made the city centre an exciting place to be at night. Especially Friday or Saturday night when we had money in our pockets, a full packet of Woodbines or Park Drives, or maybe, as a last resort, Double Ace to smoke, and girls everywhere.

After sampling some Gilmour's or Smith's or, perhaps, Tennant's in a frantic pub crawl, we would queue for the second house at the bottom of those endless steps which led up to the 'Gods'.

I'll never forget that long, brass, highly-polished rail which wound its way ever upwards following those steps because, despite the countless thousands of hands which had gripped or slid along it, it never lost its brilliance or its aura of having 'class'.

The feeling of excitement — and the crush — would increase as the first house came out, and we knew that very soon we would be in there. Sitting on one of those tremendously long, curved, plush-covered benches which filled the very roof of the place. Tier after tier of them stretching back from the wide, ornate, front of the balcony beneath which, way, way down into the darkness below, lay the 'posh' stalls.

Not for us the luxury of individual seats as they had, rather the almost obligatory discomfort of the row behind kicking hell out of your back or wiping their scruffy shoes all over your best jacket. Barney Goodman would have died if any of his 'smutter' had found its way up there.

The furtive fumblings after the lights went down at the breasts of the girl sat slightly below you on the next row down, bringing forth a mock outraged protest of: 'Gerroff . . . yer dirty sod,' which guaranteed a mixture of disgusted looks from all of her mates and laughs and grunts of: 'Go on . . . let him have a feel,' from all the lads.

Flicking the dying remains of your cigarette into a long, red tailed Stuka-dive to land, hopefully, on a big bald head far below amongst 'them'. The resultant uproar from that quarter and the consequent invasion of attendants resplendent in their long beautiful overcoats. Each one adorned with masses of gold braid and a peaked hat that would have done justice to Reich Marshall Goering.

The *artistes* on stage doing their best not to look annoyed at the loud voices arguing in the inky black, as protests and demands sallied back and forth between those pompous guardians and those which they accused.

'Oy you . . . yes, you lad . . . out . . . come on . . . out.'

'Me? . . . piss off . . . it weren't me.'

'Don't give us that lad . . . I know you . . . don't I? . . . I've had you afore for this . . . 'aven't I?'

Then another voice would join in from somewhere else saying: 'Shurrup . . . yer bleeding nancy . . . we've paid to listen to t'turn . . . not thee.'

'Who were that? . . . who worrit?' they would demand, eyes darting everywhere to flush out the hidden sniper.

'Me?' would come still yet another voice from yet another position in the darkness.

Finally accepting the obvious that no way were they going to win, they would retreat, with arms akimbo and eyes blazing to gather at one of the exits muttering amongst themselves furiously.

I don't think that they could ever come to terms with our total disrespect for their uniforms really.

It was magic up there in the 'Gods' for us. We howled in glee at the outrageous behaviour of Frank Randall as he stood there, centre stage, toothless and a mop

Chapter Five

UP IN THE GODS

of hair like a wild red bush. He'd be clad in an old army battledress without bothering to wear a shirt, or fasten his flies, and he would sway in a drunken stupour as he belched, broke wind, and openly revelled in the obscene innuendos that he poured upon the ladies before him in the front stalls.

We doubled up at the wide-eyed unbelieving looks they wore as they came out after the show, declaring loudly their intentions of writing to the Watch Committee about him.

We bounced to the big-band sound of Ted Heath with Lita Roza, and Dennis Lotis singing the *Blacksmith's Blues*. Or envied the suave panache of Vic Oliver as he wrapped the audience around his little finger.

We laughed at, applauded, boo-ed or otherwise distracted the best, and worst, variety acts that the country could offer us.

Up there, in the 'Gods'.

It was in this very theatre that Sam Duffy had finally persuaded Edna Bush, after months of 'courting' her, to take him home to meet her parents.

Later, after they were married, we all came to realise the extent of the dislike between Sam and Edna's father which, apparently, stemmed from that first meeting of the two.

To give both sides of it I would say that, if pressed, Sam would complain vociferously that Billy was impossible to please.

Billy, on the other hand, would be devastatingly succinct in his answer. If questioned about his son-in-law he would simply say: 'Who?' And any further pressing of the matter was useless, due to it being patently obvious that he refused to accept that Sam even existed, never mind was married to his one and only daughter.

The story goes that on that very first meeting Sam's appearance had the unique effect of creating a situation within that house that hadn't existed in donkeys' years.

It made Billy and his wife agree.

In fact, it made them agree with each other so completely that even they couldn't believe it either.

As far as they were concerned, the little fat figure standing before them with his best cap resting on the tops of his ears, wearing a blue pin-striped suit (the creator of which never envisaged anyone of his build trying to get into) complimented by a pair of brown boots needing a good polish, and a white silk scarf knotted around his neck, with the loose ends tucked inside the open-necked shirt, had absolutely no right to expect anyone to like him.

After the initial shock of seeing him had receded, Billy, without the slightest trace of friendliness, had enquired of Sam if he always wore a cap like the one he was wearing at present.

Taking this as an apparent agreement in his choice of headgear, Sam, smiling broadly, had confirmed that he did indeed. Whereupon his questioner had then transferred his stony gaze across to his lip-gnawing daughter to ask: 'Can't he find one that fits him?'

Now, not only did that knock the cocky grin off Sam's face, it put an embarrassed one on Edna's.

The remainder of that brief introduction was mainly filled with a pregnant silence between Edna and her boyfriend on one side of the house, and her parents showing a total disregard for both of them on the other.

Their silence spoke volumes as to what they thought of their daughter's choice.

Billy just sat there in his rocking chair, staring into the fire, whilst his wife carried on with her knitting at the table behind him, cocking her head slightly to catch the muted music coming from the old Bush radio standing inside the bay window to her left.

Edna decided to make a brave effort to improve things by relating in an excited voice that Sam had taken her to see Old Mother Reilly that night at the *Empire*.

Billy had simply leaned forward, cleared his throat loudly, and with great force spat into the burning coals, sending a huge array of steam, flame and loose ash shooting out in all directions.

'I thought yer'd brought her home with thee when he walked in,' was all that he said, without bothering to look at them.

Sam felt a sense of relief when Edna finally made the excuse that he would have to get back down the hill, otherwise he would miss the last tram back into town from Malin Bridge.

'Yer've only eight minutes left to do it in,' said Billy coldly.

'Oh, it's alright, Mr Bush,' Sam had grinned confidently as he inched his way backwards from the room, 'I could run it if I wanted to, tha' knows . . . no trouble.'

'Oh aye?' came the sarcastic reply.

'Aye,' persisted Sam, regaining his previous cockiness once more. 'I've run all t' way down Weedon Street wi'out stopping.'

An unimpressed Billy had looked at him for only the second time that night. 'Well, see as tha doesn't get too much wind under tha' cap lad . . . or tha'll be back in t' town afore that tram is.'

Then he turned back to gaze once more into the now dying fire.

'I don't like him . . . do you?' Edna's mother had remarked after the couple had left the room.

'I'd rather 'ave a fortnight in bed wi' t' mumps,' said the disgusted Billy without looking at her. From that moment on they rejected their daughter's choice, even refusing to attend the wedding at the Registry Office in Surrey Street. Edna, torn two ways between loyalty to her parents and Sam's insistence to break free, spent many tearful nights at the unfairness of it all. Anyway, she married him. And, personally, I believe it was because she hadn't got the heart to walk away.

He did his best to give her a good day, although few came, and in an uncharacteristic burst of showmanship even arranged for a taxi to be waiting for them after the short ceremony.

He felt chuffed with himself for thinking of that as a surprise for her, but Edna, delighted at the unaccustomed treat, did feel a little let down when the big black Austin pulled forward for her and she recognised the driver as being one of Sam's drinking partners. She also knew that this particular lad was also a mechanic for the firm who owned the 'bridal' car.

To make matters even worse, the lack of any wedding adornment on it in the way of flowers or ribbons was accentuated by the driver still being clad in his filthy overalls. Still, you've got to admit the thought was there.

It was what you might call a quiet 'do', and Sam felt quite proud, even if Edna was subdued. He'd got himself a wife, the promise of a little house in Salmon Pastures, and a steady labouring job in the steelworks.

As far as he was concerned, he was as good a man now as any of them.

Attercliffe Road just north of Staniforth Road junction in the late 1940s. Trams make their way past Banner's and Littlewood's, coming in from Vulcan Road or Weedon Street to town. The driver of tram number 215 is probably stamping on his warning bell at the woman trapped by traffic on his track.

Shafts of sunlight create an almost cathedral-like effect as they fall upon giant castings and annealing furnaces inside English Steel's River Don Works.

BILLY BUSH DIED suddenly on a typically cold and wet November day in 1949. He was 62, fit as a fiddle, and looked good for another thirty years at least.

How the manner of his demise came about never really came to light, all we knew was that he was found just before mid-day on Tuesday, the tenth of that month, in Molly Drabble's cellar, with only his feet and ankles showing from underneath ten freshly delivered bags of coal.

Rumours of a romantic attachment between these two (with the cellar grate being his way of slipping into her house for clandestine and passionate sessions with the widow-woman) were hotly denied by Molly. Anyway, whether it was for a bit of 'nooky', or as some others favoured a burglary lark gone wrong, or a simple case of him falling down the chute due to Molly having the infuriating and highly dangerous habit of removing the grate when she knew that Ben Kettleborough's coal lorry was coming, we will never know.

The fact remains that he was found entombed there by poor Molly when she went down to fill her bucket. Now the only light which you got down there was the bit which filtered its way down the chute, so she didn't notice the little bit of him that was on display. It was only when she stooped forward to lift by hand a particularly choice piece of best 'bright' that she felt his shoe, then his ankle, and finally the shape of his leg.

In no way could a woman of her age normally clear those steep cellar steps two at a time . . . but Molly did that day. In fact, old Mrs Flynn, who happened to be donkey—stoning her front step as Molly zoomed past her, swore that if the canal hadn't been in the way then no one would have caught her this side of Nether Edge.

It was, without doubt, a rather bizarre ending to what you might call an 'interesting' life, and provided us all with a talking point for weeks. Ben, the coalman, made

no secret of his relief when the interest value began to wane. In fact, he made it clear that the next one of us to ask for: 'Five bags, Ben . . . and put plenty o' body in 'em will tha,' would without any doubt gain-first hand experience of what poor Billy must have gone through.

Anyway, Billy was dead, and Sam Duffy was at work in the English Steel plant on Brightside Lane.

He'd spent the last four years there working in the main stores (although, to listen to him talk you'd have thought that he ran the place), and a previous seven with maintenance doing the one job without which no modern day steelworks could possibly survive — a fitter's mate. It's been said that in those long and bitter war years, when Sheffield was called upon to work as she had never worked before, it was to those men and women producing steel that the call rang loudest of all.

Well, in Sam's case, it was the general opinion, from management down to the tea-wagon woman, that if everyone had responded with *his* sense of urgency then Hitler would have been making the King's Speech at Christmas and the 'goosestep' would have been compulsory at all City Hall dances.

Sam asked for a transfer to the stores, and his manager, who couldn't sign the request quick enough, was heard to remark that had such action taken place before the outbreak of hostilities then, 'Them bloody Yanks could have stopped in America . . . and our Annie wouldn't be struggling with that kid now.'

Consequently our hero presented himself for training into the complexities of storekeeping. Within a week of starting, his new boss wondered what the hell he'd let himself in for when a deputation from the stores invaded his office and, in that brand of language peculiar to men who don't care, informed him that he should transfer our Samuel again . . . and quick.

Pointing out to these vigilantes that

Chapter Six

REST
IN
PEACE

Sam's previous job had now been filled, he was vehemently instructed to: 'Try Hadfield's . . . or Osborn's . . . Brown Bailey's . . . try bleeding Woolworths if tha's got to . . . but gerrim out of here.'

Rumour has it that in the subsequent, what you might call uncontrolled, conversation between the two managers over the internal telephone system, the intensity of their views resulted in the switchboard operator (an elderly spinster called Miss Thrush, who played the organ at St Cuthbert's but made a bit on the side doing Friday night free-and-easy's) being treated for palpitations by the works nurse.

Still, to get back to Billy.

Sam was informed at four-thirty that afternoon that he was urgently wanted at home. Or, to use his informant's vernacular: 'Duffy . . . tha's got to gerroff home as fast as them bent legs'll carry thi . . . oh . . . and your missus says tell him not to fall down on t' way.'

It was pouring down as he hurried up Janson Street, still fastening his dirty raincoat.

'Sodding rain . . . I'll get soaked in this . . . wonder what's up wi' 'em at home? I hope she's got me a rabbit for me tea . . . there's plenty on 'em in t' market now.'

All this was said aloud as he made his way up and along Attercliffe Common and into the maze of wet, unforbiddingly samelooking streets leading to Salmon Pastures.

By the time he had reached Curly Bradshaw's news and grocery shop in Washford Road, he was in a right temper.

Then it suddenly occurred to him that he hadn't had time to find out how his horses had fared that day, so he barged in. Curly had got that name by being the fanatical protector of the three long, thin hairs which lay in the centre of his shining pate.

Old Gus Fenwick, who lived two doors from the shop and was without any doubt the most obnoxious old man I have ever met, got Curly to believe that if he rubbed his head every night with a rasher of bacon, then within months he would be going to the barbers again.

Whether Curly did it or not I don't know, but after Gus spread the word every woman down there took their ration books to Mattocks butchers instead. Poor old Curly finished up with no more hair and a lot fewer customers.

Anyway, Sam barged in there, slamming the door behind him and making Curly jump and whip round at the noise.

In no uncertain terms he told our lad that he was sick of having to replace panes of glass due to people like him. Sam ignored him and reached to take a copy of *The Star* from the pile on the counter.

'I drove a bloody tank through Normandy,' grated Curly, seizing Sam's wrist to stop him having a free look, 'and didn't do as much damage as some o' you lot do to my door.'

'Well,' said Sam, tugging at the paper, 'it's a good job tha'd got some others wi' thi . . . innit? Chuffing war'd still be on now if they all drove tanks like thee.'

The tug-of-war went on during these exchanges, and it was only the door crashing again that made Curly jump once more, and give victory to Sam.

'What do you want?' Curly had roared at the scruffy looking urchin standing there, responsible for Sam getting a free look.

'Me mam says', began the frightened kid, 'Me mam says . . . can she 'ave a packet o' them dates . . . for us tea . . . and she'll pay thi when me dad gets his money on Friday?'

'No . . . she bloody can't . . . tell her what I'm trying to tell him 'ere . . . I need money to live an' all.'

'No wonder tha can't keep any customers here,' Sam said as he disgustedly threw the paper back on the pile, watching the terrified lad flee. And with Curly raving about the quality of his so-called customers he went back out into the rain, banging the door behind him.

'That's the last time I follow Templegate,' Sam grumbled, referring to the tipster in the *Daily Herald*, as he turned down the pitch-black entry which led to the yard he shared with five other families.

Entering the yard, he walked parallel to the row of outside toilets. Those narrow, draughty, freezing-cold-in-winter latrines gave birth to the universal habit amongst us of taking a bucket upstairs at night. Believe me, the daunting prospect of going out to them after dark did away with most people's æsthetic objections to the 'bucket' alternative. Tales of rats nipping your bum, or of mice running up your leg as you perched on that well-worn, freezing pot, with the wind doing its best to blow out the bit of candle you took in a jam-jar, were enough to make us turn a blind eye, and ignore the smell, when it came to using the 'bucket'.

Oh, the tales which could be told about those good friends on cold nights. However, that particular expediency in bad taste was far removed from his mind as he lifted the sneck of his back door and entered the tiny offshot kitchen, sniffing the air for a whiff of his favourite meal. Only to find it full of people.

For a start there was Ben, the coalman, face filthy from his work, and his bright red lips making Sam think of those 'nigger minstrels' he'd once seen at the *Empire*.

Alf Skinner, who had lodged with Sam and Edna for the last five years, was there, too, along with Ria Thorpe from the end house.

Mrs Flynn was making pots of tea, and Edna's mother was slumped on the old wooden chair beside the mangle, with a large handkerchief covering her face making muffled wails of: 'Billy . . . oh, Billy,' as her daughter did her best to comfort her.

Of all the thoughts which went through Sam's head, such as: 'What's her mother doing here? . . . that's her best coat wi' real fox fur on t' collar . . . she never wears that in t' rain,' or 'What's our coalman want? . . . I don't owe him owt this week;' or 'Oh, Christ . . . Ria Thorpe's here . . . I'm wet enough wi'out her opening her gob;' none took precedence over the one that really mattered.

Shaking his sodden cap so that it spattered into Ria's face, he asked of his wife: 'Did yer get a rabbit for me tea then?'

He got scant reply from his wife on that one, but the others made up for it.

Ben insisted he was blameless. Ria, in a shower of accurate spit, told him that she was organising a street collection and that Edna could borrow her big tea urn.

Mrs Flynn ignored him as she made sure that all the others got a drink of tea. Alf stood there silent with a funny look on his face that Sam didn't quite like. Whilst Rosie Crapper, who had just appeared out of the darkened front room behind Alf,

came bursting past the still wailing widow, her eyes like dustbin lids, jabbering something about what was in there which he couldn't make any sense of.

It was hopeless. All he wanted was his tea, yet what he was getting was total confusion from a load of people who, to him, shouldn't have been cluttering the place up at all.

He made a start with Rosie from next

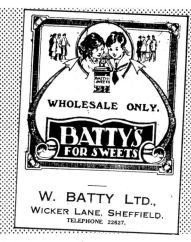

Shops on Attercliffe Road (above) and on the corner of Chippingham Street and Shirland Lane (right), where a small girl peers into the window. Is her mother inside juggling with ration books, or buying Robin's Starch or Blue Bags? This was a world of bacon slicers and biscuits bought from tins, a world without supermarkets. A world with time.

17

door. Dragging open the back door and ignoring the gibbering about Billy, and the front room, he literally pushed her out despite her pleas of: 'Listen to me, Sam . . . just listen for a minute.'

Ria viewed all this indignantly, and decided that he wouldn't be given a chance to treat her the same.

She swept past him before he had chance to see her coming, and his desperate avoiding action came too late as she snapped, 'Goodnight' into his face, giving him his second soaking of the night.

'Me and my lads 'ave collected this,' said Ben, holding out what looked to be about fifteen quid in notes. 'We all feel rotten about what's 'appened like . . . and, well . . . thought it might help...'

If only Ben knew it that little bit of 'might help' represented about six months' losses on the ponies to Sam, but before his darting little hand could reach it . . . it disappeared. However, Edna's mother managed to change hands with the handkerchief and still get to the money first, left our lad open-mouthed and Ben feeling inclined to count his fingers. 'That'll help us to buy t' boiled ham,' was all she said before disappearing behind the hanky again.

Ben left wishing inwardly that he had never set foot in that 'chuffing street', and Mrs Flynn was next. Waving aside Edna's thanks and informing Sam that 'I did it for her . . . not thee...' as he, too, offered his, she left those remaining to themselves.

There was an uncomfortable silence as Sam began unlacing his boots whilst at the same time requesting of his wife that she furnish him with full details of what had obviously been a busy day for her. Or, as he put it in his own quaintly offensive way: 'I gather your old feller's dead . . . and what's all this about Molly Drabble's cellar?'

You know, one of the truly fascinating aspects about the Sam Duffys of this world is their complete inability to grasp the basic things about themselves that have a tendency to make others explode. What, to him anyway, appeared as a perfectly innocuous way of asking what had happened very often, as now, got him into trouble due to his choice of words and style of delivery.

The newly-made widow, ignoring her daughter's pleas not to get further upset, laid into her callous sounding son-in-law with a verbal lashing that had him reeling and yelling back that 'they could hardly expect him to beat his chest in grief and despair over someone who had never missed a trick in insulting or ridiculing him.

Furthermore, he pointed out, the late, and as far as he was concerned unlamented, Billy Bush was hardly a paragon of virtue to hold up against him.

For starters, he gloated at her, how did her perfect little husband really find his way into Molly's cellar?

And so it went on between them, with Edna weeping into the hands that she pressed to her face.

Alf kept well out of it as usual, but his eyes showed the concerned feelings that he felt for Edna at having to suffer the slanging match going on in her tiny kitchen on the same day as her father had died.

It was only the great unbelieving roar of 'WHAT???' which dragged his attention back to the two combatants still slugging it out before him. He found Sam's horrified gaze rivetted upon him, and he quickly averted his own back down towards his shoes.

'Did YOU know that they'd laid him out? . . . in THERE?' Sam had demanded of him, hoarsely.

That had brought a curt nod from the lodger without him looking up to see the trembling finger that Sam was pointing towards the front room.

'In OUR front room?' came the next demand from his almost swooning questioner.

'They've put him there? . . . and YOU never said owt?'

'Well,' said the almost sheepish looking Alf with a broad shrug, 'I thought we might surprise yer wi' it like.'

Edna's mother (wearing the sort of satisfied look usually displayed by a Wigfall's collector when you paid two weeks running without missing him) found herself being roughly shoved to one side as Sam shot into the darkened front room.

Only to come to a complete dead stop at the sight of the highly-polished coffin gleaming in the firelight.

'Good God,' he groaned aloud. 'I might 'ave walked in 'ere wi'out knowing. Edna . . . come 'ere will yer? How could yer let 'em put his body in here?'

'He's me dad,' she answered softly. 'It 'appened 'ere . . . in our street . . . I thought it were t' best thing to do . . . while I fetched me mam.'

'But you've put him on our sideboard for Christ's sake,' he protested weakly. 'Who wants to see that t' first thing in a morning? It were bad enough 'aving his photo on theer . . . hey . . . hold on . . . my pools were under t' clock on theer . . . did yer move 'em?'

Once again, the underlying bitterness in that family reared its ugly head, as Edna and her mother remonstrated with him over his concern for possible monetary gain having more importance than their feelings.

Sam hit back by saying to Edna's mother (he never once in all his married life referred to her as his mother-in-law — always as Edna's mother) that if anyone should feel ashamed then it should be her and not him.

'You've no right expecting me to be happy about coming home and finding your old feller's body stretched out on our sideboard . . . all my stiff collars are in that top drawer tha knows . . . how do I get to them now? . . . eh?'

He followed that by telling her in no

Shops stand on Attercliffe Common in the 1930s awaiting demolition, the gloom and depression relieved only by posters for Libby's Milk, Palethorpe's Sausages and Gilmour's Ales and Stout.

uncertain terms that as far as he was concerned her daughter needed certifying for allowing it to happen.

'She did right,' the old girl hit back, bridling at this attack upon her offspring. 'Under t' circumstances this is t' best place for him . . . just now, anyway.'

'How do yer mean?' he challenged her.

'Well,' she said, fussing with her collar, 'it er . . . well it wouldn't 'ave been . . . well, what I mean is . . . I couldn't 'ave taken him home . . . not just now anyway.'

'Why not?' he persisted.

'Well it couldn't 'ave 'appened at a worse time,' she flustered, her eyes flicking everywhere. 'Only . . . well, what it is

like . . . Billy were decorating our front room this week . . . see? . . . and . . . well it's not finished . . . we're in a right mess.'

Now, no matter what your personality, there have got to be times in everyone's life when information reaches you that absolutely stuns all your normal senses and faculties.

For Sam, this was one such time.

I can understand the eruption of humilated fury which came from him on being told that his own front room had been designated as a funeral parlour in which would rest the earthly remains of someone whose life seemed previously dedicated to hurting him.

To be told that, and then have salt rubbed in by the widow justifying it by claiming immunity due to decorating problems was, in all fairness, asking a bit.

Well, Sam didn't like this situation. In fact, he went to great lengths to prove to the other three the extent of his dislike.

He began by kicking the old wooden chair so hard that it shot across the kitchen and hit the cellar door. He took off his dirty wet, sodden cap again and threw it at his cowering wife for being, in his view, responsible.

And then he began to swear . . . Lord how he began to swear. He swore at the coffin, he swore at Edna's mother, he swore at the lodger and at the ceilings and walls and everything else therein.

He swore with a sustained perfection that had Edna goggle-eyed, her mother making choking sounds and Alf Skinner filled, for once, with grudging admiration.

It made Rosie Crapper, who had crept back out to press her ear against the closed back door, lose the otherwise permanent grip she always kept on her ever present Woodbine, so that it fell between her opulent bosoms via the gap created at her neck by leaning forwards to eavesdrop.

Consequently we had Sam effing and blinding on one side of the door, and nosey Rosie effing and blinding on the other, what you might term a pioneer demonstration of stereophonic blasphemy.

Well, what with Sam appealing to the lodger that you just don't go around pinching front rooms for dead bodies, and the

Looking like a scene from some grim eastern bloc country, this was Newhall Road in the 1950s, looking towards Brightside Lane. Swallow Street runs off to the right.

lodger, in his usual deadpan way, pointing out that: 'She does . . . perhaps that colour coffin doesn't go wi' her new paper.'

It all came to a head with Sam demanding that Alf chase after Ben, the coalman, so that the body could be put on his lorry and 'carted back up to Stannington . . . where it should 'ave been sent in t' first bleeding place' as he put it.

Once again that night, wails, pleas and threats filled the air, complimented this time by the deeper voice of the lodger telling Sam that if he'd wanted a job like that he'd have gone to work for John Heath's undertakers, and informing the two women that expecting Sam to show any signs of distress at their loss was a complete waste of time.

'He only gets upset over his horses,' he snapped, dragging his coat off the nail in

the back door. 'Watch him when one lets him down in a double . . . it's like a visit to that wailing wall in Jerusalem.' And with a firm bang of the door he left, colliding with Rosie Crapper as he did so.

'Is everything alright?' the persistent pest enquired, as she gingerly opened the door again and let her face slide forward into the hostile environment.

Crash . . . went the half-full pint pot that broke against the door, no more than a foot from her head.

'Piss off,' bellowed Sam.

Add to that a couple of others in the same ilk, and you'll agree that Sam had little cause to feel any deeper sorrow at his former tormentor's departure.

As he saw it, when Billy went into that hole life would have one less weapon to hit him with.

THE DAYS IN WHICH he played an unwilling host to the dead Billy were a nightmare for Sam.

For one thing he detested all the house windows being covered with white sheets, as was the custom then.

For another, he refused point blank to have the traditional black diamond sewn onto the sleeve of his only suit.

And on top of these aggravations was the added problem of not getting a wink of sleep from knowing that just a few feet below him, as he lay in bed, was Billy, resplendent in that beautifully lined coffin, and looking for all the world as though he were merely enjoying a deep sleep.

Moans, groans, squeaks and rustles had always been a feature of those old houses, but to Sam they now became something far more sinister. They were the noise of Billy getting up to stretch and knock things as he took a nocturnal stroll.

Such was the strain upon his nervous system that, given the choice of that and suffering the blitz again nine years previously, he would have almost welcomed the *Luftwaffe* back with open arms.

He fumed at the way Edna's mother insisted on staying for the duration by sleeping in the attic.

'Don't say owt, Sam,' Edna had pleaded with him tearfully. 'She just wants to stop near him . . . till it's time.'

'Oh, she's welcome,' Sam had grated between clenched teeth. 'Just tell her to get in that sodding box wi' him.'

Then, mumbling something about having more bodies laid about than a Charlie Chan film, he had turned over, ignoring her tears.

Twice he arrived home from work to find the house dark and empty, due to his wife being monopolised by her mother in making the funeral arrangements.

Faced with sitting alone with a body, which his mind refused to accept as being 'really' dead, had filled him with such knee-knocking terror that he had promptly fled back down the entry as fast as he could to sit amongst the living in the *Dog and Duck*.

Not that he got any relief from it in there, mind you. Whether it was at work, in the street or in the pub, it was the same. Everyone else thrived on the situation. And if that should seem unfair, then bear in mind that our Samuel was only reaping a harvest that he himself had sown.

There were plenty down there who found him mean, selfish, bigoted and openly proud of his total commitment to his own needs first.

And they were only his friends.

No wonder that they didn't miss chances of having a stab, like Curly Bradshaw for instance.

He took the floor one night, whilst Sam was there, to remind everyone of the 'greyhound' incident.

He told of how Billy had turned up one day at Sam's with this 'bloody great beast of a thing', asking Edna if he could leave it till the following weekend, when it would be her mother's birthday.

Apparently his wife had once been to Owlerton dog track and had raved about owning one for herself.

Edna readily agreed to the surprise and waved aside Sam's misgivings. Perhaps she found a chink in his armour by saying that he never arranged a little surprise for her like that, or it might have been the rabbit that she did for his tea that night, but whatever it was she persuaded him to take it for a walk.

Sam had set off warily down our street with it trotting alongside, like a very thin Blackpool donkey, into Washford Road, over the iron bridge, along the canal bank, then joined Attercliffe Common.

Not a bit of trouble . . . nowt to worry about.

And then it saw a cat . . . a white cat, or as white as a cat could be down there.

And the cat saw the dog.

And, having seen the size of the dog, and its obvious awareness of the cat's pre-

Chapter Seven

NO GREATER LOVE HATH MAN . . .

sence, the cat showed extremely good judgement in deciding that Attercliffe Common was definitely not the best place for a cat to be at that moment.

So it ran, as fast as it could, down the busy Common.

Within seconds, our lad found himself going at a rate of knots far in excess of that for which his feet were made.

Terrified of letting go and losing this natural racing machine, he found himself taking part in the chase to catch the surrogate hare. The petrified cat, oblivious to anything except its survival, then shot across the road, followed by the delirious dog.

Now in those days Attercliffe Road was an arterial tram route to Tinsley, Darnall, Handsworth, Intake and Manor Top via Prince of Wales Road. And, as fate would have it, one of these great, lumbering structures was making its way to town from Vulcan Road. Just as this unscheduled handicap shot across the road almost beneath it, the tram-driver, quickly realising that his transport manager would want to know why he was carrying passengers underneath whilst there were still seats inside, did what all tram-drivers used to love to do. He whizzed those two big brass control handles round about fifteen times and brought the great iron horse to a complete dead stop.

Now you couldn't blame him for feeling chuffed with himself at the speed with which he had reacted, but by the same token you couldn't blame him either for tearing after Sam when one of the downstairs passengers tapped on the window of the door behind him and shouted that his conductor had just done a somersault down the stairs.

Sam, having finally dragged the dog to a halt before it followed the cat into a fishing-tackle shop, found himself roughly seized by the driver, who was shouting something about a broken collar-bone. All of which was gibberish to our lad, he couldn't even remember crossing the road.

Anyway, the upshot of all this was that Sam was fined thirty shillings for his part, plus a further ten for using obscene language to the arresting officer, and the dog never saw daylight again until Billy came to fetch it.

'Tha knows, when they collected all our gas-masks up after t' war?' Sam had spat out to the delighted Curly as everyone else laughed at him, 'Well, they should 'ave left thee thine . . . in fact, they should 'ave welded it on . . . then we wouldn't 'ave to listen to tha big fat mouth . . .' And so saying, he barged out, ignoring their calls for him to stay.

You know, if there is one element which makes your presence acceptable in a rough working-class community, it is the ability to conform. Deviating from traditional norms was asking to be an outcast, and our lad deviated that much they should have named him Robinson Crusoe.

He just didn't fit in, he felt insecure, and like most other insecure people, he covered it with an aggressive attitude towards the world. I suppose he hoped that a tough image would bring him the respect that he craved.

Unfortunately for him, or anyone else for that matter, a steelworks or a pit or a building site is not peopled by those who are inclined to appreciate play-acting outside of the theatre or cinema. Consequently, Sam found himself stuck with a rôle of his own making, which made his daily existence far worse than it would have been had he been true to himself and others.

The greyhound incident, coupled with other stories, gave those who knew him the chance to squeeze as much enjoyment as they could from his predicament at home.

Ria Thorpe jumped in straight after Sam had gone, to relate with glee, as everyone else turned their faces away and quickly covered their beer, about the time Billy almost got Sam chucked out of his house.

Actually, it was her husband, Freddie, who started to tell it, but what with his terrible speech impediment the others decided to talk amongst themselves for a bit until he had finished.

But the gist of it was that Billy wrote to *The Star* condemning all our houses as 'rat-infested cesspits', and then went on at great length to dissect the landlord, calling him, amongst other things, a 'disgusting parasite growing rich from the deprivations of his tenants'. He followed that up with the comment that were this the great Soviet Republic, then 'the scummy little Jew-boy' would be shot for the filthy capitalist that he was.

Then he signed it in Sam's name.

Being confronted later by his hysterical son-in-law waving a letter under his nose which said something about his tenancy being reconsidered, Billy insisted that he had acted simply in the best interests of his daughter.

He argued that, with enough publicity over the state of our houses, the council would perhaps speed up their re-housing programme, and then Edna would get one of those nice new council houses away from all that muck. And seeing as he didn't actually live there, he thought it should come from someone who did.

'So tha picked on me . . .' Sam had choked.

'Well . . . to tell thee t' truth lad', Billy answered him in all seriousness; 'I'd like our Edna to get one o' them new Corporation houses wi' big gardens . . . only . . . well, I fancied keeping some ducks that sees . . . and seeing as all me own's took up wi' veg . . .'

Stories of the Salvation Army turning up one Christmas Eve at the *Dog and Duck* to play carols in the tiny lounge bar at the request of a certain 'Mr Duffy', with the promise of ten pounds for their hardship fund nearly got him lynched later by the regulars.

He had found it impossible to escape, seeing as the euphonium player plonked himself in the doorway, and found himself having to hand over his Christmas bonus.

To make it even worse, the vibration from the brass section of the enthusiastic Citadel band brought down two shelves above the bar, trapping Tommy Nesbit's fingers, and Edna developed a migraine which did Sam out of his traditional yuletide 'treat'.

Lawrence Street lay between Baker Street and Zion Lane, just behind Attercliffe Road. By the 1950s the easier life had come, with a golden age of credit, motor cars, TV aerials and even a glass-panelled front door. But in Attercliffe there were still cobble-stones and gas lamps.

No blades of grass or single tree
to break the grey monotony.
No early Spring or Autumn fall
to sooth the eye or hide the pall.

Although there were pubs and local cinemas to give us a good night out, there was nothing like going into town and doing it properly. The *Gaumont* (right) was the doyen of all Sheffield's cinemas, where you could sit in a comfortable lounge until the second house began. If you could afford it - which we never could - you could dine in the restaurant. The *Gaumont* was a place to impress a girl and boost your ego . . . leaving you skint for a week!

On Charles Street was the *Empire*, (above), with the 'gods' door round the corner on Union Street, opposite Foxon's and Robinson's. An arcade ran through from Union Street to The Moor, with Sugg's and Barney Goodman's shops in it.

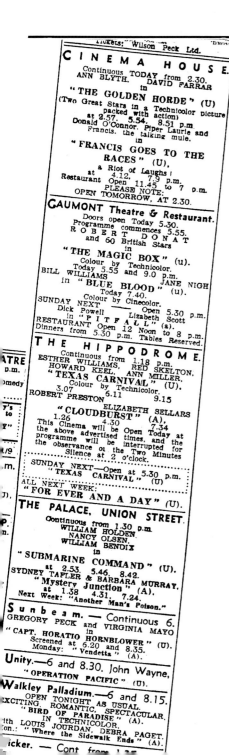
THE MORNING OF his father-in-law's interment saw Sam at work as usual. Expressions of surprise, or disgust, at his disrespectful behaviour were met with answers leaving no-one in any doubt as to how much importance he placed upon that particular event.

Entreaties by Edna and her mother fell on deaf ears, in fact they only increased his smug satisfaction at hitting back.

'I'll be there at half-past-three . . . when they bury him,' he said coldly, 'but I'm not chucking away a full day's money, not for him.'

That, as far as he was concerned, was the end of it, and no amount of tears, insults or threats that they threw at him could alter it. For once, just once in his life, he meant what he said.

True to his word, our lad duly clocked out at two o'clock that afternoon to make his way over to St Polycarp's at Malin Bridge for the ceremony. He found Alf Skinner waiting at the main gate, and eyed him suspiciously.

'I thought you were on nights?' said Sam, walking straight past without stopping.

'I am,' said Alf, catching up and keeping step with him.

'And tha's got up . . . for a funeral?' came the disgusted query.

'Aye . . . couldn't sleep anyway . . . too much going on downstairs.'

'Well, why didn't tha go on wi' that lot . . . in one o' them fancy cars?' Sam had sniffed at him.

'Naw . . . anyway, Edna asked me to come down 'ere . . . to fetch thee,' Alf had grinned at him.

'Fetch me,' Sam had pulled up to glare at him. 'I don't need fetching, kid . . . I need SENDING . . . to Middlewood Hospital . . . I must be crackers losing time over him.'

The vitriol carried on pouring out of him as they waited for the tram, and even carried on after they had boarded it.

Chapter Eight

HAS THA' SEEN HER FACE?

His mate suffered it all with a stoical silence, thrusting a threepenny bit into the conductor's hands to cover both fares into town, but as the swaying giant made its way along Saville Street, he felt a growing annoyance at the loudness of his partner's voice.

'Lower thi voice, will tha?' he finally hissed at him, aware that everyone else was listening to it. 'Tha'll 'ave 'em all thinking we're Jewel and Warris practising.'

Sam completed the rest of that journey in petulant silence at being admonished, head turned away from the annoyed Alf, staring out at the never-ending walls and gatways of Firth Browns, which stretched almost to the edge of the town itself.

Finally, reaching Castlegate, they had clumped down those twisting, steep steel stairs specifically designed to make the unwary fall, and found themselves outside the *Bull and Mouth* pub.

All it needed was for them to cross over into Bridge Street and catch another tram to Malin Bridge, except that Alf found himself being pulled into the pub.

'Come on,' Sam had insisted of him. 'I need one . . . to wash this bloody taste out of me mouth.'

Anyone living in Sheffield at that time would have told you that this particular house of refreshment was well known for its 'clientéle'. In fact, it was a standing joke that when the landlord in there called 'time' a great roar of 'No thanks, we've already had some' would wash over him in reply.

Anyway, there's our Sam, with Alf, crushed in a corner doing their best to get some beer as far as their mouths when our lad feels the bottom of his raincoat being tugged.

Glancing down (so as to ascertain just what it was making his beer slop all over) Sam found himself staring into what he considered to be the ugliest woman's face that he had ever seen.

'It's five bob,' she mouthed to him silently.

'What is?' he mouthed back, innocently.

If you should find that degree of naivety from a working-pclass lad, brought up in conditions which would normally point towards learning the facts of life at a very early age, then let me re-iterate once again that Sam was different to the rest of us.

The seedier side of life never bothered with him, it would have been wasting its time if it had. All he knew about women was that they cost you money, and that to be involved with them meant giving up other things. Like horses, for instance. As a result, Edna was the only one he had ever wanted, and the only one that he had forced himself to spend money on. He hadn't the slightest intention of making that mistake twice in one lifetime, thank you.

Which is why his puzzled gaze switched away from the frightening mess to Alf, who had wasted no time in looking the other way.

'What's she on about, Alf?'

'Don't tha know?'

'Know what?'

'She's on t' game . . . wants to know if yer want a bit up . . . for five bob.'

'Wi' HER? . . . 'as tha SEEN her? . . . she's gorra face like a bucket o' frogs . . . five bob? . . . ha, ha, ha . . . I wouldn't give our old lass that much . . . ha, ha, ha...'

The preposterous idea of actually paying, what appeared to him to resemble an accident still waiting to be seen-to, for a service which, in all probability, she wouldn't even know she was performing, almost brought Sam to his knees in mirth.

Cackling like mad, and raising his voice for all around to hear, he pointed at the two stick-like limbs protruding from beneath her tatty coat.

'Look at her legs . . . there's all criss-cross red marks on 'em at t' front . . . look . . . ha, ha, ha . . . she's been sat too near to t' fireguard at home . . . ha, ha, ha...'

The object of this contemptuous rejection slowly took hold of an empty Mackeson bottle on the table before her and began to slowly push herself upright.

'Harry . . . Harry...' she called out in a voice which truly matched her face.

Harry, over six feet tall and about as friendly looking as a combine harvester, pushed his way through to her.

'What's up, mam?'

'Him . . . that little 'un,' she rasped, pointing.

'Him? . . . what's he done?'

'Laughed at me . . . insulted me an' all . . . didn't he, Mabel?'

Mabel, her companion, whose right eye seemed to be twice the size of her left one, nodded vigorously, silently pointing at the now silent, white-faced Sam.

Why on earth that bloke ever complained about others who didn't give a toss about hurting his feelings, when he took full advantage of any chance he got to do it to others himself, is the main reason that I found him such a joy to observe.

Here again, through thinking that he was safe, he'd got out of his depth. And it showed.

Backing away so that he pressed Alf even further into the wall, he began a stuttering, spluttering, wide-eyed-innocent attempt to appease those he had just offended.

'Are tha GOING to hit him . . . or what?' demanded the blood-hungry harridan of her brutish son, who by now had begun to look a bit uncertain, seeing as his potential target was almost crying with fear.

'He's only little, mam,' he protested. 'Look at him . . . he's shittin' 'issen.' It was quite clear that even HE didn't relish the thought of taking such an unequal liberty.

Not so his obnoxious mother, though . . . she wanted blood, and size had no part in the proceedings to her.

'Mek the little bleeder even littler, then,' she screamed at him, brandishing the bottle above her head to show that she meant it.

The reluctant monster gave way and, looking almost apologetically at our lad for what he was about to do, stretched out what looked to be a bunch of white, tattooed bananas in order to seize Sam's lapels, then watched in amazement as his victim, eyes spinning in their sockets, slowly sank to the floor before him in a complete dead faint.

'How many fingers can yer see, lad?' the voice seemed to come from somewhere behind him as Sam struggled to make sense of it.

He was aware of being on his back with something rough beneath his head, and everything around him having a hazy, wobbly texture about it.

There was the buzz of voices talking, laughing and arguing as the pub carried on normally. No-one seemed to be the slightest bit bothered about a body being laid on the floor beneath them. Only the landlord cast the occasional glance his way . . . and that was just to make sure that he wasn't blocking anybody's way to the bar.

In a weak, pathetic voice, Sam asked where he was, and the same bored voice answered him.

'Tha's on t' floor, lad . . . now . . . can tha see how many fingers I'm holding in t' front o' thee?'

'No . . . no, I can't.'

'I'm not surprised wi' a cap like thine . . . come on . . . get up.'

He felt himself being pulled upright and realised that he was still in the same pub being supported by Alf and a massive copper. The officer let go to bend down and retrieve his cape, which he had placed under Sam's head.

'Tek my tip, lad,' he snapped at the embarrassed looking Alf, 'get Dick Barton 'ere outside . . . and quick. Walk 'im down to that urinal under t' Wicker Arches, cos he smells as though he's done summat nasty. Then geroff 'ome . . . both of yer. Even I don't come in 'ere unless I've got

to . . . I'm telling yer. When we raid this place and tek 'em into Water Lane nick, it's us buggers that gets into them cells . . . not these in 'ere. Now, if yer mate 'ere 'as dizzy spells like this . . . and mucks 'issen a lot an' all . . . well, tell 'im to start drinking in t' Royal Infirmary in future. Now go on . . . gerroff while I'm 'ere.'

Alf dragged the still dazed Samuel down the steps into the cold air outside.

'I feel reight bad, Alf.'

'Tha smells bad an' all,' the lodger grated at him. 'Yer chuff . . . why couldn't tha just say no to her? . . . eh? . . . that's all it wanted . . . what did tha want to take t' piss out of her for like that?'

'Who are we on about, Alf?' Sam had asked him in a confused way.

'Christ,' his mate spat out, giving him a violent shove forward. 'Tha causes all that trouble in theer . . . then tha can't even remember it...'

'Let's gerron t' tram, Alf . . . let's go 'ome shall we?'

'SOD OFF . . . I'm not gerrin' on any tram wi' thee smelling like that . . . we'll walk.'

'Worrabout the funeral, Alf . . . we're supposed to be at that bloody funeral, aren't we?'

'Forget it . . . too late now anyway . . . Jesus, if we turned up now wi' thee in this state even Billy 'ud complain.'

And so saying, Alf half pulled, half pushed the sorry looking Sam back down the way they had come.

When the two car loads of mourners arrived back from seeing Billy off, Sam kept out of the way. He knew any explanation he might put forward for his absence at the graveside, even with Alf as a witness, would be treated with disbelieving contempt.

He knew that once again he would be made to look a fool before everybody, so he stayed where he was in the bedroom, on his own, listening to voices interspersed with the sounds of plates being filled and

cups clinking into saucers.

It was cold for him, sitting there on the bed in the growing darkness, and he cursed quietly at the thought of them all warming themselves before the fire which he had stoked up on arriving home.

He wondered if Alf had told Edna yet, and her mother, about what had taken place that afternoon in the *Bull and Mouth*.

'Hope he doesn't tell her everything,' he mused aloud to himself. 'Bloody hell . . . fancy THAT 'appening at my age. Must 'ave been that red cabbage what she put on me spam for me packing-up this morning. She knows that any pickled stuff allus goes straight through me.'

Deciding that there was little point in worrying over it now, he lit yet another cigarette and went to stand before the window.

Staring down into that dismal scene, dominated by that high, grimy wall, he must have realised just how depressing it all was.

And if he did, then he must also have realised just how much worse it was for his wife living there. She had grown up to the sounds, the views and the freshness of woods and fields and clean air to breathe. To bring her here, to the soot-blackened houses and the thumping noise-ridden world of industry, was wrong. And, for once, he felt it.

Dragging hard on that fag he stood there and wished that he could make things better . . . for both of them.

Away from here, he thought, well away from all this mucky-looking street. In a new house . . . like one of them up on the Shirecliffe estate. Herbert Nish at work had got one when Fauncet Street was pulled down.

'Why don't they pull these bloody things down then?' he mused aloud at the thought of it. 'Things 'ud be a lot better for us up theer. Edna 'ud love it . . . they've all got big gardens. Owd Herbert says it's great 'aving a bath upstairs, an' t' lav's only in their porch...'

The stairs suddenly squeaked, and his melancholic daydreams disappeared to be replaced by the usual apprehension that he felt. The prospect of arguing again with Edna's mother, or trying to placate his no-doubt furious wife, made him grimace at the thought. 'Wait 'til t' others 'ave gone,' he groaned. 'For Christ's sake, wait while we're on us own.'

Hearing movements in the back bedroom made him blow out audibly in relief, it was only Alf who had come up to his room.

Stealthily creeping out, Sam crossed the tiny landing and gently tapped on the other door.

'Alf,' he whispered loudly against it, 'Alf . . . when are they all going 'ome? . . . I'm bloody frozen sitting up 'ere.'

He suddenly found himself staring into a face entirely bereft of any sympathy whatsoever for his discomfort.

'Your Edna says that she's never going to forgive yer for today. Me neither . . . I were supposed to make sure as tha got theer.'

'What about her mother,' hissed Sam, staring at him intently.

'She's not 'ere,' came the cold, curt reply, 'one of her sisters took her home, straight from t' cemetery, says she's gonna knife thi if tha ever shows thi face up there again. Don't blame her, either . . . tha'rt a bleeding disaster as far as I'm concerned.'

'Oh, be fair, Alf,' Sam protested, letting his voice raise in annoyance at everyone's disregard for his side of all this. 'I did make an effort to get theer . . . tha knows that.'

'Oh, I know that, alright, too bloody true I know,' Alf glared, 'we'd 'ave got theer an' all, except that tha can't resist a drink, then tha fainted, as well as . . .'

'Awright, awright,' Sam cut him off, 'yer don't 'ave to go into detail. I'm glad it's nearly o'er . . . might get to sit in me own front room again, when this lots finished filling their faces, that is. How much bloody boiled ham did she get? It's still supposed to be on ration innit?'

'Not when yer live on edge o' t' countryside an' know a few farmers like she does,' Alf snorted at him.

'I wouldn't go through this week again for a fortune,' Sam sighed in resignation at it all. 'An' that's another thing, innit? . . . I've lost me pools this week . . . all through him again.'

'No yer 'aven't,' Alf told him, 'I sent 'em for yer.'

Sam clutched at the flimsy bannister to stop himself falling down the stairs in his relief.

'Thank God for that, Alf,' he croaked, clutching his arm gratefully. 'I know I'm gonna get 'em reight this week.'

A grin spread across Alf's face, growing wider by the second.

'Well, if tha does,' he chuckled, 'Billy'll know before anybody else . . . I put thi copy coupon in his hand afore they put the lid on.'

Those downstairs, feasting on all that boiled ham, exchanged glances at the noises coming from above them.

Edna, to try and hide it, busied every one of them with offers of more tea, cake, biscuits, anything to draw their attention away. 'Whose up your stairs, Edna?' asked the shrew-like Aunty Doreen, sat nearest to the fire.'

'Oh, it's Alf, our lodger, he's on nights, he'll be getting ready for work,' she blustered.

'Does he talk to 'issen a lot, then?' That was Uncle Ambrose, mouthful of currant cake, and dutiful husband to Doreen.

'No . . . oh, no . . . nowt like that,' she attempted to laugh it off. 'He, er, well he's got a wireless like, up there.'

Doreen eyed her husband suspiciously. To her narrow mind there had got to be something wrong somewhere with that explanation.

Ambrose, however, flicking crumbs from his waistcoat and lap onto the floor, seemed satisfied.

'Must be one o' them sloppy plays what they 'ave on that Third Programme,' he nodded knowingly at his wife. 'They allus do a lot o' crying and wailing in them, yer know.'

I BEGAN MY WORKING LIFE learning the intricacies of bolster-grinding, double-heading, whetting and polishing with a well-known city cutler.

It was 1951, Sheffield was alive once more, despite its ugly scars from the war, and the people were enjoying a boom-time that brought with it exciting new fashions, consumer goods and fun.

Gene Autry was Hollywood's idea of a cowboy, Carol Levis presented his discoveries, and almost half of the kids in school were wearing a Gloops badge.

There were so many jobs available in the 'sits vacant' columns of The Star that they filled two complete pages in small print; and cinemas? . . . there were dozens of them.

I worked a five-and-a-half day week, got paid thirty shillings for it, and received ten of those back in spending money.

It was the year that I saw teddy boys for the first time, and marvelled at their audacity in dress and DA haircuts, it was the year that I realised a long-held dream by owning a Claude Butler bike for a fifty shilling deposit and a four-and-sixpence a week payment to Sugg's sport shop.

None of your Wigfall's gas pipes for me, thanks, I wanted one that would take me all the way to Mablethorpe . . . and it did.

There was me and Harry Owen, who worked in a brickyard and got nearly three quid a week, and Pete Fairfax, too.

He was a trainee fireman then, on the LNER, and used to brag to us about all the different places that he'd been to. Still had that same problem with his stomach-churning nose that he'd always had when we were kids, though, and God knows how the senior fireman and the driver coped with looking at that all the way to Edinburgh.

We sent the tent and a lot of other stuff on ahead by rail, then set off through Tinsley and up Bawtry Road, determined to get there under our own steam, and we did.

We cooked lousy meals on a tiny meths stove that we had bought from Millington's Army Stores, got thrown out of every pub that we tried for being under age, and did our best to sing like Guy Mitchell or Frankie Laine every time that we saw any girls. Then gave it up when we realised that most of the girls could imitate these two top singers far better than we could.

Herbert Lee, another one of our childhood gang, couldn't come with us, he'd been dragged off to Blackpool with his parents to stay in one of those posh boarding houses. Mind you, his dad worked down the Nunnery pit, and his mother was the chief usherette at Darnall Cinema, so they could well afford to pay the twelve-and-a-tanner a day that it cost to live it up like that. All the same, I bet we had far more laughs than Herbert did.

It was the time when Attercliffe Common catered for everything that you might need without you having to go into town for it. Banner's Stores had an escalator and a unique system of suction pipes which whisked your money away in a small round tube up to the cashier's office. Two minutes later, it would clatter back into the basket placed beneath the return pipe with your receipt and change in it. You didn't have to go walking around then looking for somewhere to pay, or stand well back in apprehension from flashing, bleeping space-age tills.

Boozers? Well, if you could make it from Norfolk Bridge all the way down to Weedon Street, having a drink in every one along that stretch, then you could DRINK, mate.

I wish that I could have a pound note for everyone I know who tried it. Most of them finished up with faces that changed colour more often than the Belisha beacons that they kept on walking into.

It was the time that Sammy Gregory, who was two years older than I was and had always been the 'cock' of our gang, got his call-up papers. He passed his medical as A1 at the recruiting centre on

Chapter Nine

AND THEN THERE WERE NONE

Ecclesall Road, told them that he wanted to be a tank driver in the *Third Hussars*, and got told to mind his own business, as he would be joining the *Yorks and Lancs*, then dropped bow-legged when his orders and railway warrant arrived to find that they were going to make a cook out of him instead.

'Ah thought tha were gunna be a tank driver?' snotty Pete Fairfax had said to him, as we all stood talking to him in a group that night.

'Ah did,' said the morose looking Sammy, 'ever since ah took t' papers out for Curly Bradshaw. It were him what told me all about 'em tha knows . . . he were one . . . went to France on D-Day him, tha knows.'

'Ah bet that's how he lost all his hair, then,' Harry Owen giggled.

'Naow, he got that from scratching it every time he were asked owt,' laughed Pete, making that same old vile noise with his nose, as he made that equally vile piece of green elastic disappear once more.

Personally, I couldn't understand why they had told Sammy that he would be joining the *Yorks and Lancs* and then put him in the *Catering Corps*.

'Don't ask me, kid,' he said miserably. 'If I knew t' answer to that one . . . well . . . I'd know why that doctor looked up me arse, wouldn't I?'

We only saw Sammy once more after his call-up, due to us going to Mablethorpe that summer. He'd finished his basic training and had come home on a forty-eight hour pass. We all made a big fuss of him in his uniform, with his beret stuffed under his epaulet, and envied him like mad. He looked healthy and fit, and obviously enjoying every single admiring look that he got from the girls who saw him.

We asked him a million questions, and didn't like most of the answers we got back.

But, all the same, I envied him that uniform and its bird-pulling power. He told us that he was about to start a course on cooking, which would take him through until September, and then he was hoping to be posted abroad to do some 'real soldiering', as he called it.

'I've told 'em,' he said assertively to impress us, 'I want the Far East — Hong Kong, Singapore . . . owt like that. Heard about them women out there, tha knows . . . our drill sergeant were theer, told us that he had four one night . . . while he were on guard, at that. Christ, I shan't 'ave t' strength left to boil an egg, ne'er mind do any cooking for 'em.'

Obviously, all this had the rest of us goggle-eyed with delicious hallucinations about our own impending call-up and the possibilities of sampling those oriental goodies.

We talked for what seemed hours that night on the corner of Salmon Pastures and Washford Road, re-living all the growing up days that we had shared.

Sammy had been the best 'scrapper' for miles, he'd looked after all of us at school and in the streets, and now he was off. Perhaps to the other side of the world which excited him so much.

I remember feeling uneasy at the thought of him not being around with us anymore, of realising that growing up meant much more than leaving school and getting a wage. It meant much more than smoking fags in the street, staying out a lot later or swearing with the men at work.

It meant the end of something, too, like all the daft kids' pranks that you play on dark nights to annoy the grown-ups, or the comfort of knowing that your dad will protect you if somebody bigger threatens.

It was Sammy standing there in his uniform that I envied which brought home to me at that early age that the gang, the life and the fun that we had shared was almost over.

He came home again in August, but we missed him with being on our holiday at Mablethorpe. He saw all of our parents before he went back, and left word that he had got his wish to serve where he desperately wanted to go, the Far East. Only it wasn't those mind-blowing places that he had raved about to us, it was a place called Korea, wherever that was. There was fighting there, but it was mainly the Americans who were involved in it.

Anyway, Sammy went out there and found himself attached to the *Duke of Wellington's*. Then about three weeks before Christmas he got himself killed when the convoy carrying supplies that he was in came under Chinese artillery fire.

'Sod that,' was Herbert Lee's first reaction. 'Ah'm going in t' Navy, ah don't care what them women out theer are like . . . yer don't get across many when yer dead.'

Thankfully, on our part anyway, that war ended well before our papers arrived in 1953.

But as I left the Midland Station on the train to Catterick to join the *Royal Signals* for my own service, I was extremely conscious of the fact that Sammy had done all this before me.

I was going to wear that uniform, do things that I had never done before, see things that were new to me.

Somehow, after what had happened to Sammy, I didn't feel as excited by it all as much as I had done two years before, when we had seen him for the first time as a soldier.

I was on my own now, as were Harry and snotty Pete and Herbert Lee. Our gang was finished, we were all grown up, and Salmon Pastures was somewhere back there in the rain.

The B & C Funeral Parlour stood at number 3 Attercliffe Common twenty-five years ago. Just a few doors up was the *Tramcar Inn*, but no-one was put off their ale. You could hire the upstairs for the wake, and a decent funeral wouldn't have set you back £100.

In cramped and draughty workshops, and with only hand-tools and the minimum of mechanisation, pocket-knife cutlers sent Sheffield's name around the world.

I HATED the cutlery industry for its smug self-satisfaction of world fame that hid the often atrocious working conditions which produced the very source of that title. The grease and dust and fumes, the huge dangerous belts running down from the main shaft high above you, driving the spindles which held the various stones or mops that you leaned over to do your work. It was a dirty, repetitive and often dangerous job if you let your bored mind drift onto other things.

At first, as a boy straight out of school, I admired the quality of the work that I watched being produced. Slowly, however, that admiration waned as the reality that life must hold more for an inquisitive youth just embarking on his adulthood than a daily quota of blades to be finished without letting your imagination extend any further than that.

I suppose that Sheffield, or anywhere else for that matter which has made itself famous for a particular product, can count itself lucky to have access to the type of person who is willing to forgo any latent talent that he or she may have lying dormant within them to do the tasks which result in those who employ them basking in the accolades which come their way.

Personally, I never had any desire to help create an egotistical mantle of quality which the factory owner could parade before his business friends if his only claim to such ownership was that he employed you. As I saw it, and still do, he had no right to take the credit for something that he couldn't do himself.

I shed not a single tear when Her Majesty extended a cordial invitation for me to join her forces As far as I was concerned, they should have sent for me much earlier.

Whatever my rather sour recollections may be as regards those first three working years of my life, I would not extend those feelings to include the people that I shared them with.

I will always feel grateful to that marvellous band of women who did the buffing, because their earthy, crude approach to all of life's taboo subjects brought those very unmentionable things into their proper perspective. Sex was something to be laughed about, and God help you if you blushed easily.

They taught me that false airs and unjustified claims about yourself can often leave you exactly where you deserve to be, looking a fool. And they proved it the first time that I tried to get clever with them, by removing my trousers and liberally daubing my rather underdeveloped Bishop with dolly-grease.

Apart from the fact that I nearly died of embarrassment at what they were doing to me, I crawled out of there feeling lower than a snake's belly at the laughs and remarks that they made concerning the limited potential of the equipment with which I had been endowed.

'Christ . . . is that it? I've got thicker string round me apron than that.'

'Hold 'im still, Fanny, if I catch 'im too hard wi' edge o' me ring he'll 'ave to start wearing knickers. Now, if thi mam asks who did this, tell her I did, lad . . . for being bleeding cheeky. Tell her from me that if that doesn't start developing soon, then I'll 'ave it to clean me ears out with.'

I defy anyone to undergo the ordeal of having their nether garments removed by a gang of no-nonsense females, have the tenderest part of their anatomy blatantly handled and greased by hands rougher than a bear's bum, whilst being continually reminded of its failings, to have any remaining misconceptions about male superiority. That is a myth, and I thank all of them for releasing me at a very early age from a burden I can well do without, thank you.

Then there was Wally, who had been working there for so long that the boss couldn't even remember setting him on. He must have been well into his eighties when I left, and I wouldn't be surprised if

Chapter Ten

MADE IN SHEFFIELD

he was still there yet.

He had the habit of putting his pipe down anywhere, and then totally forgetting what he'd done with it.

He was almost blind, anyway, and to read the *Telegraph* at dinner break he used to don a pair of spectacles which had lenses so thick that everyone swore that they had been cut out of a disused aquarium at Belle Vue. He set the place alight three times by plonking his pipe down amongst cotton waste, and was a positive menace as he groped his way around trying to find things.

Really, his only use was his vast knowledge of the trade through being a Master Cutler for so long. He'd forgotten more than anyone else there knew. Mind you, you could extend that to include his flaming pipe.

I heard more than one woman give him a mouthful as he stumbled around with his gnarled old hands before him, searching everywhere for his beloved pipe.

'Wally . . . that's my leg what tha's got hold of, tha knows,'

'Eh?. Ah'm looking for me pipe.'

'Aye, well tha'll not find it up there, yer dirty old sod . . . try Winnie further on. She likes to hide things.'

Good old Wally. He taught me that it sometimes pays to act daft.

There was Pat, who worked in the warehouse on the etching machine, always had a nice shy sort of smile for me whenever I took the trays of blades in there. She lived with her family on the Arbourthorne estate in one of those pre-fab things, and was about my age. All the other women used to shout out to her as I came in, and we'd both go as red as beetroot whilst all the others had a good laugh at our embarrassment.

She was a nice lass really, if a little on the plain side, and I did eventually ask her out on condition that she kept quiet to all the others about it.

What I remember most about that night is the amount of lipstick that she had put on. It was that thick that I'll swear she had used their core rake to apply it. I took her to see James Stewart in *The Springfield Rifle* at the Wicker Picture Palace, and came out looking like one of the Indians in it.

We went out a couple of more times, but then she started making silly noises about me going up to meet her parents some Sunday, and that was enough for me, thanks.

My mind at that time was on getting away from Sheffield altogether, and I had no intentions of getting myself bogged down with Pat, or anyone else for that matter. So, if she was formulating any sort of long-term plans with me in mind, well, all I can say is that she wasted a hell of a lot of her lipstick.

Still, all the same, I'm grateful to her, because in the short time in which we shared back-row seats and draughty doorways she helped me to dispel the memory of those caustic descriptions of my legacy. In fact, were it possible, knowing what I know now, for me and those great buffer women to re-enact that little scene, I can sincerely assure them that I would now simply lie back and think of England, gladly.

They were three years in which I learned a lot from, and about, people. Most of it is gone now, and what is left I would imagine will bear little resemblance to the industry that I knew.

The countless stairs that I climbed in Charles Street, Matilda Street, Eyre Street, Rockingham Street, and all the other streets which criss-crossed that area and was a complete warren of little shops owned by little Mesters, each one of whom continually urged their small workforces on with repeated cries of: 'Are they done yet? . . . C'mon . . . they've got to be out for Friday.'

All of them working like the clappers to meet deadlines set by the big cutlers who paid the piper, and therefore called the tune. No, it was an experience for me, that's all.

On the day that I pressed that red stop-button on my machine for the last time, I knew that my involvement with cutlery had come to an end.

It's importance now is minimal, having passed into foreign hands, and the area it covered has been altered to meet modern needs. But it is an important part of Sheffield's history, and I am glad that I was able to see it at first hand before it was too late.

So, to all those of them that clipped my ear, kicked me up the backside, performed unmentionable things upon my personage, and generally reminded me that I was just a kid who hadn't 'done nowt yet', let me say that you may have been replaced by a multiplicity of machines which are 'cost effective'.

But, by heck, they'll never turn out the blades that you lot did.

I THINK OUR CITY FATHERS have always been very conscious of all the grim, depressing images that those eastern approaches to the Town Hall have presented to outsiders.

I mean it was easy for them to justify the muck and noise and smoke in the days of unlimited work, wasn't it? They could always hit back at the 'Dirty Sheffield' brigade with proud boasts about our importance to the nation, our world renown for steel, our vast contribution to the wealth and safety of this land.

It was easy for the effete South to look down their noses in disdain at us, but where would *they* be without our industry. And so they silenced our critics with facts, but they couldn't change the image. We WERE a dirty city, and for all their indignation they couldn't hide it.

Well, they don't have to now, do they? Go and have a look for yourself some time. When I look around those vast empty areas now, I find it hard to imagine that it is the same place that I knew as a child and a youth.

They've put trees down there now in parts, and grassed the open wounds. Ye gods, we had to take a long tram ride to see those wonders of nature in my time. The air is positively alpine to the filth that we breathed, and it's so QUIET.

Ah well, England doesn't need us so badly now, so we can wash our face. We can even have those City Fathers of ours claim that we are the cleanest industrial city in Europe. I'm not surprised, seeing as the part that made us the dirtiest has been obliterated. Good riddance to it, it has no part in modern times, with its inadequate housing and its soot and its outside toilets that freeze up every winter.

The great steel Goliath has met its economic David, and now lies dead.

So, to look back now and think of what it is that I want to remember, then it has to be the people. The characters.

Ria Thorpe in the end house, born with a water sprinkling system fully installed within her mouth, long before such things became available to park-keepers.

The very first woman in Salmon Pastures to own one of those new-fangled television sets. I can see all of us now, stood there gaping up at that huge 'H' ariel that had suddenly sprouted from her decidedly dodgy chimney stack, as though it were the visitation of some alien being that straddled her roof looking for victims.

She was so chuffed to be leading the field with this rather crude forerunner of what we use today, that she even left her curtains wide open at night, knowing that there would be about fifteen of us all crowding her window-ledge trying to get a look in at the jumping picture. I don't know why we bothered.

It didn't come on until five at night, then went off again at six. Back on again at eight until final close-down at eleven.

We'd be pushing and shoving and climbing all over each other in our attempts to squint through her faded net curtains, for what?

It had a twelve-inch screen, enough 'ghosts' on it to frighten Boris Karloff, and had poor old F . . . F . . . Freddie try his best to play hell with her for the six bob a week payment that he found himself lumbered with. By the time he could manage to ask her what would be on that night, they'd be playing the National Anthem.

Anyway, after about a week, she put a stop to our free show when she realised that her front windows were getting ten times muckier than anybody else's, and Freddie decided that he preferred his corner fireside seat in the *Dog and Duck* of a night.

'Hey up, Freddie; can't keep away from us then?' Sam Duffy had bellowed into the fed-up husband's face.

'Ah'm not . . . not . . . not . . . ah'm not . . . ah'm not deaf . . . ah'm not deaf, that knows . . . ah'm not deaf just 'cos . . . just 'cos . . . ah'm not deaf just 'cos ah

Chapter Eleven

WHERE SPARROWS COUGHED

can't . . . 'cos ah can't . . . chuffing hell . . . 'cos ah can't talk reight.'

You know, to be fair, Freddie had a valid point in chastising Sam. Everybody seemed to shout at Freddie because for some strange reason, just because he had this terrible speech impediment, they automatically assumed that his hearing was impaired as well. I don't know if you have noticed it or not, but a hell of a lot of people shout at the blind, too.

Poor old Freddie stuttered very badly, and got a lot of earache as a result of it.

So, Freddie returned to the fold, leaving his besotted wife to pay homage alone to that new addition to the working man's ever-increasing standard of living.

He met all their good natured ribbing stoically and gave as good as he got . . . eventually.

As he said, what was the point in paying six bob a week to sit staring at a small glass window behind which there appeared to be a continual fall of snow, when you only had to wait until January and see it for nowt.

Well, about a week later, the spell must have released its iron grip upon Ria, too, because she marched in that night with Freddie to claim her old seat once more.

Naturally, she came in for some stick from the regulars about showing off and wasting Freddie's money, which would be far better spent on bottles of Guinness for her and so on.

'Yer'll all be getting one soon . . . now that yer've seen ours . . . yer will . . . we don't have to go to t' pictures now . . . we've got us own . . . yer'll all have one soon . . . yer will.' All that was splattered out at them, accompanied by a determined set of her mouth and a wagging right forefinger.

Tommy Nesbit, the ragman, had somehow overlooked his close proximity to Ria, and paid for it. The left side of his face, head, his ear and neck took the full brunt of the spray.

'For Christ's sake...' he said, taking off his cap and beginning to dry himself, 'give us your key Freddie. If she's gonna sit in 'ere every night again, I'll watch the bleeding thing for yer.'

Then there was Rosie Crapper, who tried to organise a street trip to London for the Festival of Britain, and no one would go with her.

'It's only nineteen and six on t' train,' she kept saying.

Grief, the replies that she got made me cringe. She even tried to tempt old Gus Fenwick as he was buying some Vick vapour rub in Curly Bradshaw's shop. Glutton for punishment that woman, no one else would go anywhere near him. I detested him, his house was on my paper round, and don't I know it.

He had a dog, a Jack Russell terrier, and believe me that never were two of God's creatures more suited to each other than those two were. All terriers have an inbuilt urge to fight, especially Jack Russells, but that varmint was evil.

Anything that moved . . . it bit it.

They reckon that a red-hot piece of coal fell out of Gus's fire one night and the little sod had it before it knew what it was doing. Gus said that he had never seen it run up his curtains before.

I remember once, in a rather pathetic attempt on my part to gain its doubtful friendship, and hopefully eliminate the nightly terror I had of getting to know its teeth, I rolled up Gus's evening paper and offered it to the miniature shark. It made one vicious snap at it, ignored Gus, who was standing behind in his doorway, and set off like a cat with its arse on fire down Washford Road.

It obviously thought that it had acquired a bone of gigantic proportions, and I have no doubt that it fully intended to bury it safely somewhere along the canal bank.

I can only insist that any other fourteen-year-old, as I was then, subjected to the abuse and dragging about that I was,

interspersed with cruel clouts around the head from a very hard cap, would have done exactly what I did that night; I ran home crying, leaving the bag of undelivered papers lying where I dropped them.

Curly Bradshaw was furious when he learned that thirty-odd customers were sat that night without their paper, and charged the whole lot to me. As a result, I finished up working all that week and received the princely sum of eightpence instead of my usual five bob.

So you will excuse my rather tainted views on old Gus.

Anyway, there's nosey Rosie pestering old Gus to go to London with her, and him giving her his famous 'monkey look' and wasting little time in telling her the exact part of her anatomy best suited for putting it before turning back to snatch the chest ointment from the counter and demanding of Curly: 'Does tha know owt about wirelesses?'

'I know that yer put ornaments on 'em,' Curly had cackled back.

'Is that why tha sits on yours?' Gus had growled.

Curly quickly realised the he was playing with fire in trying to be funny, so he abandoned that idea and played safe by asking what the trouble was.

'Won't come on,' the toothless old mouth snapped, 'been like it a week now. Ah'm missing Henry Hall's Guest Night . . . it's Hutch what's on toneet. Smashing singer him, tha knows. Will tha come and 'ave a look at it?'

'Me?' laughed the nervous Curly.

'Aye, thee. Tha were in t' army weren't tha?' said Gus in surprise at Curly's reaction.

'Course ah were in t' army . . . but I drove a tank. Yer don't plug them in, tha knows,' protested the uncomfortable shopkeeper.

'Tha sells this for bad chests . . . but tha'rt not a doctor, either,' Gus had shouted at him as he waved the jar beneath

Curly's nose and looked at him in contempt.

Then he barged Rosie out of the way and dragged open the door.

'Can tha imagine Churchill trusting him wi' a tank?' he had snarled at the open-mouthed woman. 'Ah wouldn't trust him wi' my toasting fork. Huh, been in t' army an' he can't fix a wireless . . . he's useless.'

'Well, rub some o' that bleeding Vick on it then,' Curly had screamed at the old man's disappearing figure as he tore around the counter to slam the door.

Yes, there was only one of Gus . . . thank the Lord.

Molly Drabble, the unfortunate widow-woman who had found Billy Bush buried underneath her coal, got married again.

He was a bookies' runner called Maurice Burns, but some wag or other, because of Maurice's surname, christed him 'Fats'. Consequently Fats Burns became something of a standing joke down there, and more than one fell for it when they were asked if they knew 'Fat Burns'.

'Course ah know fat burns,' Sam Duffy had snapped in disgust at the query, 'Christ, what a daft question to ask anybody. Has tha ever had any on thi hand?' Then looked about him in amazement as everyone else in the bar laughed.

Well anyway, Molly married Fats, who used to stand on the corner of Fauncet Street taking illegal bets and stuffing them into a bag that he carried, which had a clock device fitted to its neck to time the placing of the slip.

She left us and went to live with him in his big council house on the Wincobank estate, but kept in touch by regularly calling down to see Mrs Flynn, her old long-time friend. Then about nine months after the wedding, we got to know that poor old Fats had been involved in a particularly nasty accident which had meant him having to pack in his regular job as a fettler at Firth Browns.

Seems like her new husband, a keen rose-grower, had got himself well and truly damaged when he couldn't resist dashing out of their house with a bucket and shovel to lay first claims upon a veritable mountain of manure freshly delivered by an extremely thoughtful corporation horse, which they used in those days to pull their dustcarts.

Now, so intent was Fats to be the first to get his implements, if not his hands, into this natural, and free, fertiliser, that he didn't even wait for the great beast to move off first. He just dived under the shafts and began shovelling like a Californian gold miner.

Well, whether he accidentally caught the massive animal with his shovel, or whether it just happened to be the type that is given to nervousness at the thought of something going on beneath its tail which it couldn't see, I don't really know. But Fats finished up somehow jammed beneath the cart axle with his bucket laid in a front garden three doors down.

Molly, obviously distressed, related all this to Mrs Flynn after visiting him later in the City General Hospital, where he had been admitted for a broken pelvis and suspected double rupture.

'He'll be lucky if he does any more fettlin' then,' the old woman had sympathised, and you can imagine how that particular comment was taken when repeated to the likes of Sam Duffy or Rosie Crapper. Anyway, old Mrs Flynn proved to be right, because Fats, what with his injuries and being into his late fifties, was unable to resume that very strenuous job, and had to take a much lower paid job there as a washroom attendant.

'Sod that,' Billy Whittaker had remarked to Alf Skinner, as he handed over a pint to him in the Dog and Duck. 'If that's what yer get for growing roses . . . well, ah'm glad we 'aven't got a garden.'

Alf had just sort of given a resigned shrug and commented that it was one of those things in life.

'He wanted that horse muck, so he took a chance. That's it,' he said.

'Took a chance?' Billy gaped, 'tha wouldn't get me giving any bloody corporation 'orse any chance to ruin my wedding tackle, mate.'

Ria Thorpe had been listening to all this from her corner seat beside Freddie, and couldn't resist joining in on it.

'Ah wouldn't be upset if I were Molly,' she shouted over. 'She's got a nice 'ouse now, 'asn't she? That's better than any wedding tackle I know. I'd swap his any day for an indoor lav,' directing that last remark at poor old Freddie, and accentuating it with a derisory look and a jerk of her thumb.

Alf had simply given Billy a disgusted shake of his head at her crudeness.

'Know what?' he said softly.

'What?'

'Ah'm surprised that tha doesn't get a bleeding rainbow in 'ere whenever she's in.'

Old Mrs Palmer, the one who steadfastly refused to sit in the vicinity of Ria after catching a cold from the incessant spray, lost her husband Ben around that time, too.

The old pair of them had lived in Salmon Pastures more years than any of us, and always swore that they wouldn't move, even if the council came to pull them down.

They'd had three kids in that house, and lost two of them. One, a little girl I remember, died in Lodge Moor Hospital of diptheria, and a son of theirs was killed in North Africa during the Second World War.

That had left them with just their Albert, and he did well by working his way up on the Town Hall staff to become something of a boss in the waterworks department. The old girl was delighted about it, and took great pride in telling everyone about the lovely house that he had bought in Fulwood.

Now, Ben must have been in his seventies then, and had always been noted for his somewhat extreme carefulness with his money. I know it's a solid fact that he used to mix dry, used tea leaves with his pipe tobacco, and I dread to think what it must have done to his lungs. I don't doubt for one minute that the unusual additive extended the life of an ounce of Shag, but when he lit up it tore your nose apart just to smell it. If the aroma got inside your house, everybody would start looking behind sideboards or under settees, convinced that a stray cat had got in and done something nasty somewhere.

Ben was the only bloke down there who could make Billy Whittaker open the pub windows. And that is going some when you consider that open windows then let far more smoke in than they ever let out.

Well, the old lad must have been drugged out of his mind on that mixture, because he was sucking on his pipe when he jumped off a tram at the bottom of Staniforth Road, and then calmly walked beneath an SUT coach on its way to Filey. Ben died as a result of multiple injuries, but the pipe escaped unmarked.

Everybody missed old Ben, he'd been a tower of comfort and strength during the blitz. He proved to be untouchable with his stirrup pump, as he whizzed everywhere he was needed during those bad nights.

By the time Jerry had finished with us, Ben had perfected his skill to such a degree that he could put incendiary bombs out before they landed, never mind did any damage.

But, as Curly Bradshaw said, if only Ben had been inclined to spend a bit of his money then, he just might well have been *on* that coach to Filey instead of giving it a close inspection from underneath.

Ah well, it takes all sorts to make a world.

Anyway, when the old girl recovered from losing her Ben, and began taking her place again in the pub, the other women were quick to note that her new handbag was somewhat larger than the old one. Not only that, they were puzzled at her continual stroking and patting of it as she sat there behind her usual bottle of milk stout.

Well, it goes without saying that it was Rosie Crapper who discovered that Ben may have been dead, he may also have had a very proper and very effective cremation, but, thanks to his fiercely loyal wife, he was still very much resident in his beloved Salmon Pastures. Wrapped up in her bag. And where ever Mrs Palmer went, Ben went, too, including the *Dog and Duck*.

Well, you can imagine the queasy, and in many cases offended, looks and comments which came her way after that. Poor old lass suddenly found herself enjoying about as much popularity as a leper would in a baby clinic.

What with Ria spraying 'em in the best side, and her frightening 'em to death sat there in the dram shop, Billy Whittaker was spitting rivets. Mind you, to be honest, I wouldn't have fancied sitting opposite her trying to enjoy a pint knowing that old Ben, or what was left of him, was laid in her lap squinting up at me every time I took a swig.

'In her handbag?' Sam Duffy had gaped when Edna told him. 'Yer mean she's sitting in theer at night wi' him in her bag? Christ Almighty . . . I thought it were two bags o' crisps what she'd got in theer. I don't know, there's some funny buggers down 'ere, alreight. She wants to send half of him back to Brook Bond's after what he smoked.'

Of course, Billy Whittaker had to do something about it.

As Gus Fenwick complained, in his usual pleasantly venemous way, 'It's bad enough having to pay tenpence a pint in 'ere, tha knows, wi'out 'aving to worry about whether she'll drop that bag. I don't want him floating around on t' top o' me ale, not at this price.'

So, reluctantly, Billy Whittaker had the task of insisting of the old girl that as much as he had valued her, and Ben's, longstanding custom, he just couldn't allow what she was doing to continue.

'Sixty years he lived down 'ere,' she sniffed tearfully at him, 'sixty years . . . through two world wars . . . risked his life for this street . . . allus spent his money in 'ere.'

Billy had grimaced at that, but let her carry on.

'Nowt could drag him away from 'ere when he were alive, nowt. And he's not going now, either, not wi'out me. That's why I had him cremated. I know it's only his ashes but, well . . . he's still 'ere . . . do yer see, Billy.'

I reckon that you'd have needed a cast-iron heart to listen to that from an old and very miserable woman not to have felt any sympathy for her. And Billy, despite some rotten ways, like putting your change down amidst all the beer slops which seemed to have permanent residence on his bar, *did* feel sympathy.

He cleared a shelf beneath the bar especially for Ben's remains, and told the old girl she was welcome to carry on coming in anytime she pleased. So long as she deposited her bag with him to keep in 'Ben's Den' as he called it, until she was ready to go home.

'I hope tha does t' same for me when I'm gone,' scowled Gus.

'Oh, no,' Billy grinned wickedly, 'I've got just the place for thee.'

I CAN'T EVER REMEMBER feeling any need to show more than the obligatory respect for Christ's teachings than that demanded by our school head.

To me, as a lad, and almost everyone else that I knew, it seemed to be inconceivable that a young mind should concern itself with the scriptures when there were so many other far more exciting things to wonder at.

As a result of this perfectly logical conclusion, prayers in the morning assembly were dutifully intoned in monosyllabic fashion so as to satisfy Mr Langston, surrounded by his sour-faced staff up there on the stage, whilst letting one's mind dwell upon things of *real* importance.

Such as whether Gordon Wragg would keep his promise to swap his cigarette card photo of Sam Bartram, the famous England goal-keeper, for your spare one of Raich Carter. Or whether Jeanie Bolan *really* was as easy to feel at as Harry Owen kept on excitedly insisting she was.

Quite honestly, I didn't look upon this order of preference as being in any way disrespectful to the faith into which I had been baptised. More as, well, getting your priorities into a sensible order. Consequently, any heartfelt prayers that I ever felt that I should offer up unto Our Lord were usually in relation to divine direction being given to Dennis Woodhead's left foot as he raced down the wing for Wednesday before pin-pointing a perfect cross for Derek Dooley to head in the winning goal.

The fact that this manouevre didn't always have the same delirious conclusion, often resulting in Wednesday losing the game, made it patently obvious to me that God only listened when he wanted to. Not necessarily when you needed him. Either that or he was consumed with jealousy by us making football of a higher importance than Himself.

Verily, therefore, was He, His churches and His minions mocked from all sides of our temple at Hillsborough.

Insults hurled at one's own team for their failings, or at the other lot for their 'dirtiness' or at the myopic imbecile in charge and his 'bleeding flag-waggers' always seemed far more penetrating if heavily laced with theological overtones.

Hence a player in one's own team, if caught in possession and losing the ball, could expect something like: 'For Christ's sake part wi' it will tha. Tha'rt tighter than t' Pope's wife.'

Now this may have shown the renderer's ignorance in matter's Catholic, but it was certainly effective in making the offending player feel like missing the next home game rather than be laughed at again by forty thousand heathens.

Likewise, should the goalkeeper make some elementary blunder which resulted in 'them' scoring, you would see his head and neck do their utmost to burrow down twixt his hunched shoulders as a loud raucous voice would emanate from the crowd behind him on the Kop to declare: 'Yer big pillock. Our vicar saves more than thee.'

Blasphemous, I agree, irreverent beyond redemption, but who cares when your team's losing.

Little wonder, then, that Bryn Thomas, the Reverend of Carbrook parish, within which lay Salmon Pastures, considered his esteem amongst us to be on a par to that which we reserved for the nit nurse.

Apart from christenings, weddings and funerals, you would have had more chance of getting us to visit Bramall Lane than his grimy black church. Not that he didn't try, bless him, but it must have been heart-breaking for him when he surveyed his Sunday congregation and counted approximately one person for each year of devotion that he had given to us. And when I say that he spent eight years with us you'll be forced to agree that it was hardly worth pumping the organ up for.

No wonder he walked around with a permanent look of dejection on his thin, elongated face. Trying to get eight people to

Chapter Twelve

STRANGER IN PARADISE

lift the roof in exaltation, whilst knowing that the forty pubs or so within his jurisdiction could hardly cope with the crush, would have disillusioned the Archbishop of Canterbury, never mind a little Welshman.

Being Welsh and typically full of eloquent religious fervour didn't help him much either in the land of constant overtime. What with having doors shut in his face by harrassed mothers worried about the washing they'd left on the fireguard to dry, or being stonily ignored when he took to visiting pubs in a desperate attempt to get *somebody* to at least have a look at the inside of his church, well, his heart must have bled for his valleys and all those lovely singing Celts.

No, hawking Jesus door-to-door like the latest pan-scrubber and pub to pub, and even inside the very steelworks themselves, only served to make Bryn Thomas feel less wanted. It did absolutely nothing in the way of making us more pious.

But, you know, although I admit to never being a churchgoer, I never believed that this made me less caring than those few kids amongst us at that time who actually went to Sunday School or sang in the choir, and were generally looked upon as being 'goodies'. Personally I resented the unfairness of that comparison.

I mean, Tommy Jessop in our class was in the choir for four years and he was a born varmint. I watched him one day trap Betty Clitheroe in a corner of our classroom when the teacher was out and force a live newt down the neck of her jumper. Talk about pandemonium. She covered every corridor screaming her head off, and Mrs Allsop had to rush her to Dr Hudson on Attercliffe Common to stop Betty going into a fit.

I wouldn't call that being good.

Betty's dad didn't, either. He went round that night and broke their front window trying to get Tommy's dad to come out and fight. How that kid could stand angel-ically singing hymns at weddings and carol services, whilst his twisted mind dreamed up other little giggles to play on the likes of Betty Clitheroe, simply makes a mockery of the term 'good'.

In 1952 Bryn Thomas left us to carry on alone with our ungodly ways. He just simply gave up competing with Desperate Dan in the comics, Dick Barton on the wireless, draught bitter, and the Durango Kid at the Attercliffe *Globe*. Poor old 'Taffy' hadn't a chance in that sort of company.

He became the chaplain of Cardiff Prison, and if he couldn't get a full house in there then he deserved to be de-frocked.

I hope he did, get a full house I mean, for I'd like to think that he had the pleasure of hearing his favourite psalms fill his new chapel. He went without it long enough in Salmon Pastures.

And I'm sure that those grim prison walls couldn't have been any more depressing for him than the dirty old church that we gave him. No doubt he would find the majority of his new parishioners just as apathetic towards him as we were, but at least they would come to his church, listen to his sermons and praise his God in song. They would, by their enforced attendance, do something for Bryn Thomas that we had been incapable of doing. They would give him back his purpose in life.

I hope that he spent many happy fulfilling years 'inside'. And if he is alive now and knows that Salmon Pastures is no more, well, I just hope that he blames it upon economics. And not upon our sins.

By the 1960s Attercliffe was beginning to disintegrate. The trams had gone, along with some of the back streets, and works buildings were beginning to crumble. By the 1970s not even God could halt the decay: Carter's was on Attercliffe Road at Salmon Pastures, whilst the Zion Congregational Chapel and Sabbath School were on Zion Lane.

THE ONE MAN that I always felt great respect for was Alf Skinner. In fact, I would say that he alone held the respect of everyone living down there in Salmon Pastures.

And yet, like all the rest of them, he was just an ordinary working man. Nothing special at a glance, cloth cap and overalls, yet . . . different. He was tall and gaunt with a serious, almost disdainful, look about him that could quite easily have been off-putting.

Unless you took the trouble to notice his eyes. That was where the *real* Alf Skinner lay. They were greeny blue, and so expressive of what he inwardly felt, even though his outward features invariably denied it.

I admired him tremendously for the way in which he would not follow the pack. Would not blindly adhere to the traditional and often ridiculous norms by which the rest of us all lived.

He knew that they felt edified by merely getting his response to them. And I'll bet my bottom dollar that deep down he must have felt totally justified and satisfied within by it.

He was, if you remember, the long-term lodger of the Duffy's, having joined them at Sam's insistence on returning to work at the English Steel Corporation in 1944.

After suffering serious back wounds when the destroyer that he was serving on took a hammering from the Germans, he had spent a year convalescing in a naval hospital down in Devon, before being discharged as unfit for any further service.

Anyway, he was then dumped into the lap of the Ministry of Works, who wasted little time in getting him back to his native Sheffield to make use once more of his pre-war skill as a fitter. They fixed him up with grotty lodgings in Glossop Road due to his former home in Darnall, along with his mother and two sisters, being blown away in the blitz. Then, like the Navy, they promptly forgot all about him.

Perhaps it was because of what he had been through, or perhaps it was because I never once knew him to seek any sympathy for it, that he stirred something inside me bordering on idolatry. Whatever it was, I'll swear that Sam Duffy and many more down there secretly shared what I felt.

Anyway, he came to lodge in Salmon Pastures after meeting Sam, who at that time was still employed as a mate in the maintenance shop prior to him transferring to the works stores.

And Sam, having been discarded by everyone else in there, wasted no time at all in fastening on to Alf.

It goes without saying that Alf didn't need very long to realise that his previous luck in life was in no desperate hurry to change itself for the better, but, being the type that he was, unlike all the others, he didn't complain as he suffered Sam's idleness and incompetence. Meaning that he virtually did everything himself.

Now Sam, feeling grateful that his new carrier hadn't turned out to be a back-stabbing management lackey like all the rest of them, repaid Alf by insisting on him leaving his miserable lodgings and moving in with him and Edna to make himself at home in their attic.

It would be like telling a fairy story to say that they all then lived happily ever after, because they didn't.

Even Alf had a breaking point. But for all of that, Alf kept him as a mate at work. And Sam kept Alf as a lodger.

Personally, I believe that Alf formed a great affection for Edna, although I could never imagine him taking any advantage of the situation. No . . . I think after seeing her husband's inadequacy both at work and at home that he felt sorry for her. And from that a sense of responsibility for her well-being. Perhaps even for the both of them, who knows?

I think that Alf knew that they both felt more secure by him being there with them. And again, perhaps, he welcomed it as an

Chapter Thirteen

JUST ANOTHER DAY

outlet for the loss that he must have felt for his own family. So he stayed, much longer than he had ever intended doing. And the two men developed a comical love-hate relationship which delighted everyone else.

There was one incident that I remember so well, with Sam, as usual, getting the worst of it.

It originated at work one morning, when Alf was driving out the stubs of some old bolts which he had just burnt the heads off in a cover plate that had been brought into the shop for him and his mate to repair. Cursing vehemently beneath his breath at the sight of his 'mate' sitting a few feet behind him studiously considering that day's racing page, he banged away with hammer and drift at the stubborn stubs.

Now technically, if Sam had been doing what he was being paid to do, that's to say the work that Alf was now unwillingly engaged in, then he would not have been in line for the perfect trajectory which the hammer-head took when it decided to part company with its parent shaft. But, things being as they were, Sam *was* sat there. And he was in line. And it didn't miss him, either.

Alf was left staring blankly at the now useless piece of wood in his hand, and his idle mate slowly submerging feet first beneath the 'snap' table, wondering all the while why he should feel like he suddenly did.

Somehow, and I wouldn't have liked to attempt it myself, Alf had half carried the glassy-eyed and gurgling Samuel across the yard to the ambulance room for the nurse (a rather unfeeling creature called Annie Frost, who bred ferrets) to point silently at the treatment chair into which she wanted the carcass placed.

I have a theory that pain is relative to the strength of the sufferer's mental capacity to withstand it, which accounts for the continual barrage of noise emanating from our lad Sam, as he gingerly touched at what felt to him like a miniature balloon on the side of his right temple. Couple that with the periodic rotation of his eyeballs and various combinations of facial contortions, and you have some idea as to what hard-hearted Annie and the sheepish-looking Alf had to watch.

Annie, never one to burden herself with any pretentions of gentleness, decided that it was time to go to work, and without any further ado made her usual preliminary examination by gripping Sam's face firmly by both cheeks and giving the lump several vicious pokes all around its extremities. At the same time uttering that classic of all ridiculous questions: 'Does that hurt?' What is it about her sort that makes them drive others daft by asking the obvious?

Anyway, there's Sam slumped in the chair, convinced that he was now going to die without ever backing the Derby winner, and baffled at the musical notes bouncing around inside his head without any proper sequence, and Annie Frost clumsily dabbing masses of iodine on his lump, with Alf not knowing whether to stay or go back to his broken hammer. So Annie decided for him.

'Hold his head still, will yer,' she snapped, adding, 'I'm putting more on this chair-back than I am on his bloody lump'.

'It's burning me,' whined Sam.

'Burning yer?' she rasped into his screwed-up face. 'Course it's burning yer . . . it's meant to bloody burn yer.'

'Why?' he moaned, forcing the question out through lips pursed from the pressure of Alf's grip upon each side of his compressed face.

'Why?' she shouted at him, banging still more of the fiery liquid onto his pulsating lump, 'I'll give yer some why, I will that . . .

From Staniforth Road Junction (with Attercliffe Road) trams ran to town, Darnall, Tinsley and Firth Park. In 1948 (looking towards town) a Bedford ex-Army lorry stood outside Wigfall's shop whilst men in flat caps and women with baskets join the ghosts of my early years.

open yer gob again and yer'll not be able to ask why. Now, shurrup while I see to yer.'

Sam closed his eyes and obeyed.

Alf had a job keeping his face straight when the pair of them finally emerged back into the yard. The sight of the wobbly Sam, head swathed in yards of bandage and his mucky cap perched atop, tested every ounce of his restraint to keep from making things any worse by laughing.

Anyway, following Annie's directive, the pair of them set off to see Dr Hudson on Attercliffe Common to have Sam's head thoroughly looked at, with the injured party leaning heavily upon his unwilling mate and loudly declaring that the aforesaid nurse would be much better employed staying at home pegging a rug than inflicting herself upon those in need.

Now old Dr Hudson was probably the most well-known figure in the whole of the East End. In fact, I think that he helped deliver the most of us. I remember him as a stern-looking man, lightly built, who as the years passed grew progressively more hard of hearing. Yet, despite his increasing age and his difficulty in understanding just what it was that you had come to see him about, he refused to retire.

I remember that one of the standing jokes about him was that he could only listen to his favourite Tommy Handley on the wireless by pressing his stethoscope against the speaker. I'm sure that Mrs Mopp, Funf, Colonel Chinstrap and all the rest of that programme would have had a birthday with him had they known.

Anyway, in rolls our Sam, looking like Prince Monolulu, followed by his embarrassed mate causing all the others already waiting to gape at Sam's raddled head.

'Ooh, ah say,' one grey-looking old hag croaked at him. 'That looks bad . . . does

The Moor in the early 1950s was a mixture of gaps and little shops. This is Moorhead, and the solitary bus crosses the present-day site of the dual-carriageway.

it hurt thi much?' She finished off by pressing her filthy hankie to her mouth to stifle another rasping cough.

Sam had simply given Alf a despairing look at what he considered to be obscene stupidity.

'Ignore her,' Alf said, straight-faced. 'I think it's Annie Frost's mother.'

Well, they sat there for ages awaiting Sam's turn and listening to the bellowing voice of old Hudson in the other room. And I *do* mean bellowing. Believe me, the ethic of having your doctor's confidence certainly didn't apply in our practice. That was the price that you paid with old Hudson. Either that or suffer.

And poor old Percy Denton *must* have suffered. For he endured the agony of having numerous piles for four years rather than see Hudson and have everyone else know about it. The trouble with that, though, was that the longer Percy hid the truth about his condition the worse things became for him. Until, eventually, he was walking around like an overweight Gordon Richards, and his wife refused to go out with him anymore until he was 'seen to'.

Yes, Hudson did his bit in creating pain as well as curing it. Anyway, back to our two awaiting their turn to enter the echo chamber.

'Name?' yelled Hudson without looking up, as Sam seated himself before the big old oak desk.

Sam winced visibly at the blast and squeaked: 'Duffy'.

'WHAT???' came a second ear-full, this time making Alf jump as well.

'DUFFY . . . SALMON PASTURES' Sam hollered back, pulling a face at the increased throbbing of his lump.
the little bit that he could see of it.

'Who put all that on?' he yelled, pointing with his fountain pen at the huge dressing.

'Annie Frost . . . at work,' Sam muttered.

'What???' came another ear-splitting blast.

At this point Sam had turned to plead silently for some help from his nervous mate standing behind his chair. And Alf, avoiding Hudson's quizzical gaze and shuffling his feet on the threadbare carpet, did his best to explain Sam's predicament.

'Well,' he began, 'I was using this hammer at work, see, and...'

'Using a what??'

'HAMMER,' Alf yelled, then snapped aloud, 'Christ . . . tha's got me at it now.'

And so it went on, with Alf yelling out his explanation and Hudson yelling back across the desk for him to repeat this or that, and with Sam sat between them both gently stroking the blue-black-red lump which seemed to pulsate more painfully with each shout.

Finally he put a stop to the noise by tugging fiercely at his mate's sleeve and pointing to his bandaged head whilst shouting as loudly as he could: 'Show him . . . just show the deaf old sod, will tha. I feel ten times worse now than before I come in 'ere. Show him . . . and let's go back to work. It's quieter theer.'

And that's just what Alf did. He removed the dirty cap, took out the over-sized safety-pin fastening the dressing, and proceeded to half fill old Hudson's surgery with more bandage than the doctor had used in his entire working life.

Then, to our lad's horror, he was once again subjected to a series of sharp pokes all around his newly-acquired appendage, as old Hudson closely examined the wound, silently determining the amount of damage done and possible after-affects. Until, with a final grunt to signal his satisfaction, he straightened up and retired back behind his desk to start fishing in one of the drawers.

'Right,' he barked, making Sam jump again. 'Drop your trousers.'

Now it's my firm belief that there is nothing more calculated to generate fear into any man than being told by someone in the medical profession to perform this particular manoeuvre. Because, without exception, the odds are that the recipient of such an order will feel silly, embarrassed, and above all else very, very vulnerable.

Which just about sums up our Sam's reaction to it, signified by the look of unadulterated alarm which he shot at his somewhat surprised mate. Alf in turn just shrugged and looked away.

'It's me head,' Sam hissed at him, 'why does he want me to drop me kecks?'

A larger shrug came from the uninterested Alf. Then, straight-faced, hissed back: 'Perhaps he wants to see how far down that lump goes.'

Sam turned away in disgust, then went an even whiter shade of white at the sight of old Hudson holding the hyperdermic up to the window to catch the poor light coming through the dirty panes.

'Good God Almighty,' Sam groaned, feeling every remaining vestige of energy quickly drain away from him. 'Just look at the size of that needle. He's never gonna stick that in my arse, Alf . . . not all of it . . . surely.'

His mate was grinning from ear to ear at the thought of what was about to happen.

'Put thi cap back on, Sam,' he chortled, 'I don't fancy seeing that point as it comes through t' top of thi head.'

Sam closed his eyes and tensed himself as old Hudson advanced. For years afterwards he would insist that he didn't know how he came out of that surgery alive.

The massive lump on his head, coupled with the excruciating discomfort of his penicillin-flooded bum, made each step agony for him. He grumbled, complained and generally made Alf feel like a criminal at what had befallen him that day.

The Common was busy as usual with shoppers, and each accidental knock that Sam received brought forth a further demonstration of histrionics from him, in which he described in details that grew more crude with each collision the origins and breeding of those too clumsy to avoid his suffering body.

His lump pulsed away like the Eddystone lighthouse, his backside felt as though old Hudson had used a brace-and-bit, and he felt sick.

Alf bore it all in his quiet tolerant way as, with the pathetic-looking Sam leaning heavily upon him, they slowly made their way back home to Salmon Pastures.

His thoughts were a mixture of annoyance with himself for being the one holding the hammer when it broke, frustration at the fact that if his idle mate had been doing his job then he wouldn't have been sat in the flight path of it, and self-consciousness at having to play nursemaid to the bandage-cocooned, stiff-legged, complaining idiot who was drawing everyone else's attention to them both.

Perhaps that's why they didn't see the pram. Perhaps each of them was so wrapped up in their private thoughts that nothing else existed for them at that moment.

Whatever the cause, they didn't see the pram.

And the girl pushing it didn't see *them* either. Here again, perhaps she, too, was fed up of pushing the damn thing and of the squawking kid inside it.

Perhaps that is why she no longer cared about others making their way all around her on the crowded pavement. She just pushed it, and took it for granted that others would move out of her way.

But our two heroes didn't, did they? No, of course not.

They didn't because the crowds were just a blur to them. And they were both far too busy with their private thoughts.

It was only when one of those sharp chrome struts that held up the pram hood gouged itself deeply into Sam's groin that the awareness of other things returned.

Now, I always think that there is something slightly degrading in seeing a grown man reacting to pain as a young child would. The open mouth silently working away, the saucer-like disbelieving eyes and the rapid finger-pointing movement at the part that hurts.

That was Sam. On his knees. On Attercliffe Common. Amongst the watching crowd. Not a pretty sight with his bandaged head and both hands kneading away between his legs, causing the women looking down at him to look away in distaste.

Not a single word of sympathy, mind you, or apology from the girl for what she had just done. Just a stony glare which questioned our lad's right to get in *her* way. She just set off again at the same furious pace, with the pram like a lethal battering ram before her, leaving the remains of her attack to its fate.

Sam was finished. How much can the human frame take in one day? Head banging, backside in flames, and now his unmentionables somewhere deep inside him. That was it, he couldn't go on, not another painful step.

So Alf dragged him bodily into Banners' doorway and propped him up against their hardware window to set off and walk the remaining two hundred yards to Salmon Pastures, where he borrowed the decrepit wooden trolley that Gus Fenwick always fetched his bags of coke from the gas depot in Effingham Road with.

And that, believe it or not, is how Sam finally arrived home that day. With all of us kids running alongside, cheering and laughing. And Alf manfully pulling away at the length of rope attached to the front, with his fat little mate tucked up inside the box, eyes closed, hands tightly pressed between his legs.

It was VE Day all over again for us.

Pity that Sam couldn't join in on the fun.

Cambridge Street in the 1950s was home to the *Hippodrome*, the Trades & Labour Club, Brown's Outfitters, McDonald's Hairdressers, and that notorious mecca for Sheffield's teddy-boys . . . the *Barley Corn*.

Cambridge Street, Site of Bethel S.S. and Chapel. May.1959.

ONE DAY THE politicians and economists and sociologists will get round to explaining the causes and effects of the decline of this once-great industrial city. No doubt they will trot out a bag full of facts, figures and graphs which will answer our astonishment at those huge gaps which have appeared in the East End and then sit back feeling well-chuffed at the way in which their trained minds have put us all in the picture. Except for one thing . . .

You do *not* wipe out a longstanding way of life simply by flattening its location. It remains while-ever there are those who remember it.

Sheffield has had to endure an enforced metamorphosis, as though she were some giant snake shedding its old skin. Unfortunately, however, thousands of working lives lay trapped within her cast-off and, unlike the snake, she will be a long time in accepting her new look. Her greatest industry has all but gone. Victim to, amongst other things, a political dogma which sees little further use for that which once made this country a world power. The push-button age has arrived . . . sweat is out of date.

Having said all that, and seeing as all my efforts have been concentrated on looking back fondly on what *was* rather than moralising on what now *is*, I would prefer to indulge myself in recalling some of the things familiar to my generation . . . once upon a time.

Like the resonant voice of Raymond Glendenning on the wireless. And how we sat tensely listening to his nerve tingling rhetoric as he described the fights of Bruce Woodcock, Freddie Mills, Randy Turpin, Sugar Ray Robinson and all those other boyhood heros of the ring, Or gave us a stride-by-stride account of the majestic Derby. He painted verbal pictures of Stanley Matthews, Gordon Richards, Don Bradman and many more, by sheer power of description. Nowadays it takes millions of

pounds worth of TV equipment and people like David Coleman. He gets so excited, he sounds as though he's crying.

And what about those newpaper advertisements urging us to try 'Bonomints . . . the wonder cure for constipation.' Load of rubbish. Everybody down our way took Syrup of Figs. A dollop of that could make an elephant run. The finest test of your potential speed of reaction to sudden shock, was to find yourself sitting on the outside toilet when someone else in the family had just been given a dose. Believe me, the rate of knots which they employed coming across that yard in search of relief would have graced Concorde. Your own needs were forgotten in your haste to get clear before they literaly took the door off its hinges. I reckon they should have issued blue touch paper with every bottle of it. Good old Syrup of Figs, the original conception of the binary principle. One . . . it moved *you*; two . . . it shifted every bugger else as well!

At home we had those great Yorkshire Ranges, heated from the coal fire and black-leaded into a dark brilliance. Add the skill of the women who used them and you finish up with Yorkshire puddings an inch thick, enclosed within a ring of high peaks so crisp you had to break them off and soak them in your gravy to save cutting your gums.

And glorious new cakes which swelled into life on the hot- plate behind the oven door. The very smell of them, and the sight of your mother with a towel protecting her hands as she gingerly removed them and lined them up on the window-sill to cool, made your taste-buds dance. Then finally, smearing the inside of them with thick dripping from the roast . . . magic! If one fell on your foot you'd be off school for a week. But who cared? Keep your curries, king prawns and pizzas . . . gimme me mam's new cakes.

Teddy Boys introduced us to a style and colour in clothes far removed from the

Conclusion

WHEN THE WIND BLOWS

limited spectrum that we had always known. They showed us full draped jackets in dazzling hues, with velvet collars, which fell all the way down to fasten at a point just above the knee. Drainpipe trousers with ankle-grabbing ten-inch bottoms, finished off by luminous socks in those massive crêpe-soled wedge-heeled 'brothel-creeper' shoes. Top it all off with a 'DA' haircut, heavy duty rings on your middle fingers and an inexhaustable supply of Wrigleys spearmint and you had an ensemble that we called *STYLE*.

They got drunk, got into fights, showed total indifference to the older generations scorn and showed the rest of us of that age that the world was changing. They danced the 'bop', whirling and twisting their girls so that those flouncy skirts flared to waist level, revealing stocking tops held up by suspenders. You could go blind on a good night.

I remember how silver sixpences were sometimes employed by the girls as a makeshift repair if a suspender button should break. And I'll never forget the immortal observation on this practice, that should you be lucky enough to get your hand that far, then at least you'd have your tram fare home. Sad to say, in my case, I walked more than rode.

What about the way we'd sit reading those little squares of newspaper stuck on a nail behind the lavatory door? Bet your life the piece you were looking for had already been used by some previous occupant. Still, there was one thing to be said for that primary type of toilet paper, it gave most of use the chance to show what we thought of Hitler.

Then there were those tiny, infuriating, copper needles which we fitted into the pick-up heads on the radiogram, fumbling and cursing as we went down on our knees for the umpteenth time to search the carpet after dropping it again. And if it happened to land on one of those pegged rugs which all the women used to make by cutting up all the old coats in the house, then you might as well sell your records. No way would you ever find it in one of them. I've known babies get lost in one.

I wouldn't mind, but when you did manage to fit a needle it would be worn-out in less than a dozen records and you had to suffer it all over again. Mind you, to be fair, the discs in those days weighed half-a-ton each and were at least an eighth of an inch thick. Try carrying a dozen sometime and see what I mean. I reckon that Wilson Pecks are to blame for half of the people of my age who walk about with a decided limp today.

One bloke I will never forget is Larry Bates, who was our barber. I can feel him now standing behind me after he had finished depriving me of most of my hair. And smothering what bit was left in Brilliantine. 'Larruping' he called it, as he pummelled your skull. You got out of that chair convinced that if only on technical grounds he had to be guilty of some sort of assault. He refused point-blank to consider any other style except the one which *he* deemed to be proper, that is, a short back-and-sides.

A very sour man was our Larry. Never carried on a conversation with us young'uns, drove you daft by breathing heavily down his nose on your head and neck whilst he was working, and definitely wouldn't sell 'gentleman's requisites' to anyone he suspected of being unmarried. I know, because Harry Owen, one of our gang, asked one day when we were getting cropped. Larry laid into poor old Harry as though he were to blame for the Don being mucky! We all said, 'Sod him' after that and started going to MacDonald's in Cambridge Street.

There were the nights we flinched in our seats in the *News Theatre* in Fitzalan Square, as the 'Three Stooges' committed impossible acts of violence upon each other. Whilst the Duke of Darnall paraded elegantly along Attercliffe Common complete with gloves and spats. Geoff Duke burned the roads up on his Norton winning those famous TT races on the Isle of Man. Followed by George Formby doing it much more safely on film. He even managed to play his bloody ukelele on the way round. Meanwhile, Flash Gordon escaped a million different deaths in his battles with the Evil Ming every Saturday afternoon, as we ate 'tanner' Dairymaid choc-ices. We got carried away by alternate boos and cheers as first Johnnie Mack Brown and then the outlaws took turns in filling the screen in wild chases which saw thousands of bullets fly. If ever the Yanks run out of lead, blame him, and Roy Rogers and good old Hoppalong Cassidy.

Mind you, I always thought that there was something out of place with Roy Rogers. He always sang those lousy songs to his horse 'Trigger', rather than to Dale Robertson who always took the female lead. I could be wrong.

We all brought the *Reveille* for the pin-up on the front, and *Picture Post* gave us close up views of Johnnie Ray's contorted features as he poured his heart out singing 'Cry' in his own tearful and distinctive way. He'd have one hand covering his right, (or was it his left?) ear to hide his hearing-aid and had all the girls wetting themselves in hysteria long, long, before the likes of Elvis or the Beatles ever got near a stage. Todays multi-millionaire bi-sexual freaks may think that they are original and innovative, but they're not; no more than the 'Prince of Wails'.

It was the time when pubs shut at 10 pm sharp and the nearest thing to a nightclub was to take a few bottles home for a sing song. There were no cinemas on Sundays or Good Friday because it was considered sinful. Not that it made any more of us go to church mind you; it just went towards making a miserable Sunday even more miserable when you were too young to go into a pub and the cinemas were shut.

Ten-bob notes had a comforting feel